THE LORD'S DAY IN SCRIPTURE

THE LORD'S DAY IN SCRIPTURE

Rodney D. Nelson

RESOURCE *Publications* • Eugene, Oregon

THE LORD'S DAY IN SCRIPTURE

Copyright © 2019 Rodney D. Nelson. All rights reserved. Except for brief quotations in critical publications or reviews, no part of this book may be reproduced in any manner without prior written permission from the publisher. Write: Permissions, Wipf and Stock Publishers, 199 W. 8th Ave., Suite 3, Eugene, OR 97401.

Resource Publications
An Imprint of Wipf and Stock Publishers
199 W. 8th Ave., Suite 3
Eugene, OR 97401

www.wipfandstock.com

PAPERBACK ISBN: 978-1-4982-8125-6
HARDCOVER ISBN: 978-1-4982-8127-0
EBOOK ISBN: 978-1-4982-8126-3

Manufactured in the U.S.A.   AUGUST 29, 2019

CONTENTS

Introduction | vii

1 Whatever Happened to the Lord's Day? | 1
2 The Lord's Day in Post-Christian America | 10
3 The Lord's Day and the Jewish Sabbath | 17
4 When Was the Resurrection of Christ? | 26
5 The Time of the Resurrection and the Lord's Day | 49
6 The Lord's Day in the Acts of the Apostles | 66
7 The Lord's Day and Christian Stewardship | 74
8 The Lord's Day in Revelation 1:10 | 79
9 The Lord's Day and the Pagan Sunday | 92

Appendix 1 The "Fixed Day" in Pliny's Letter to Trajan | 107
Appendix 2 A Response to Ranko Stefanovic's "'The Lord's Day' of Revelation 1:10 in the Current Debate" Andrews University Seminary Studies 49.2 (2011) 261–284. | 120

Bibliography | 133

INTRODUCTION

THE Lord's Day is not a topic that most Christians esteem as highly important in their faith journey. The phrase itself is not mentioned by most Christians due to Sunday being the most dominant and recognizable term for the day of Christian worship and fellowship. Then why write a book about a little used phrase for a day? In sum, it is important because much is packed into this phrase that is very significant for Christian identity and purpose. Following are some discoveries I have made about the Lord's Day that have significantly impacted and strengthened my faith and may do the same for others as well.

The Lord's Day is the day of the Lord's resurrection. The Bible never commands Christians to observe the Lord's Day. It was on the Lord's Day that the "third day" predictions of the Lord's resurrection were fulfilled (Luke 24:21). It did not occur on any other day of the week. The resurrection of Christ occurring on the first day of the week was no coincidence. It is a day when Christians can celebrate the triumphant resurrection of Christ over sin and death having accomplished salvation for all human beings.

The Lord's Day is the historic Christian day for worship and assembly. The Lord's Day was not only the primary day for Christian worship in the early church but has been throughout Christian history. By gathering for worship on the Lord's Day, Christians of all ages stand together confessing the event that occurred on that day, the resurrection. The resurrection is the central event legitimizing the claims of Christ and the Church (1 Corinthians 15:12-19). The Lord's Day provides Christians the opportunity to worship God celebrating the greatest act of salvation history.

The Lord's Day is a day that belongs to the Lord. The term "Lord's Day" only appears in Revelation 1:10. The Greek term used for "Lord's" means "imperial" and "belonging to the Lord." This indicates the Lord's Day belongs to Christ and his Lordship is demonstrated by virtue of the resurrection (Revelation 1:10-18). Similarly, the "Lord's Supper" (1 Corinthians 11:26), belongs to the Lord. It is his meal. While the Lord's Supper regards the crucifixion (1 Corinthians 11:26), the Lord's Day regards the resurrection (Revelation 1:10-18).

The Lord's Day reminds Christians to take God seriously. The resurrection of Christ that is commemorated on the Lord's Day is both celebratory and reverential. Most of all, the Lord's Day signifies the triumph of Christ over death! The Lord's Day reminds Christians in worship to take God seriously because he completed salvation on the Lord's Day.

Finally, the Lord's Day reminds Christians that God reveals Himself in scripture by mighty acts of redemption. Scripture reveals the fulfillment of God's promises of salvation in the resurrection of Jesus Christ. The Lord's Day reminds Christians that God's salvation was revealed and acted out in history. The resurrection on the Lord's Day is the great historical confirmation of God's providence in the salvation of mankind. When Christians worship on the Lord's Day they testify to the authenticity of the Bible and celebrate God's triumphant act in world history. The Lord's Day is the day upon which God vindicated the salvation accomplished by His Son.

The Lord's Day needs a rebirth of focus in the Christian Church. If it is merely a day Christians have off work, the Lord's Day will merely be an empty shell of significance for Christians. The heart of Christian worship on the Lord's Day is the action of God on that day and the possession of it by the Lord. More than any other factor, gathering for worship on the Lord's Day, with renewed sense of focus and understanding of the day itself, may renew the life of the Church on the Lord's Day.

It is my prayer that this study might renew an appreciation of the resurrection as an act of God on the Lord's Day, and what the day commemorates.

1

WHATEVER HAPPENED TO THE LORD'S DAY?

EVERYONE has heard the venerable saying that history forgotten is history repeated. Equally true is that meaning is lost when history is neglected. This especially applies to the Lord's Day in the modern Christian world. Few traditions of the Christian Church are as universally recognized and as universally neglected as the Lord's Day. Ask the typical Christian what the Lord's Day means to them and the reply ranges from informed insight to apathetic ignorance. The Lord's Day simply does not carry the significance it once had in the lives of Christians.

Four Distinctions

Christians in the early church did not worship on the Lord's Day because they were commanded to. There is no evidence the Lord's Day originated from a decree handed down from Jesus or the apostles. Observance of the Lord's Day is one of the dominant traditions in Christendom, yet, unlike many Christian customs, the tradition arose lacking Biblical injunction. The origin of the Lord's Day as a Christian day of worship is "in many respects obscure," yet the recognition of its existence in the New Testament bears the "stamp of canonical authority."[1] Apostolic stamp of ap-

---

1. Bauckham, "Lord's Day," 240.

proval should not be confused with apostolic decree. The Lord's Day has been observed and understood at least four different ways throughout Christian history. They are the Lord's Day associated with the pagan Sunday, as a rest day, a sabbath day, and as a civil Sunday.

The Pagan Day of the Sun

The first association is the Lord's Day and the pagan day of the sun. The term "Sunday" stems from pagan roots, not from Christian origins. The first usage of "Sunday" in Christian literature was made by Justin Martyr in his *First Apology* (ca. 152 C.E.). He refers to it as "the day called Sunday."[2] Justin called it Sunday because he was addressing the Roman emperor Antoninus Pius. Justin identified the Lord's Day as Sunday so the emperor would understand on which day Christian worship took place. He did not refer to the Lord's Day by name. Nor did he call it Sunday because Christians addressed it that way. Another text discussing Sunday was written by Tertullian in his *Ad Nationes* (ca. 145–220 C.E.). The text was written to address charges made by pagans and others that Christians were sun-worshippers because of their gathering to worship on Sunday. Tertullian spared no words in denouncing such a charge:

> Others, with greater regard to good manners, it must be confessed, suppose that the sun is the god of the Christians, because it is a well-known fact that we pray towards the east, or because we make Sunday a day of festivity... It is you, at all events, who have even admitted the sun into the calendar of the week; and you have selected its day, in preference to the preceding day as the most suitable in the week... (Y)ou who reproach us with the sun and Sunday should consider your proximity to us.[3]

---

2. Justin Martyr, *First Apology*, 67 (*The Ante-Nicene Fathers* 1:186).
3. Tertullian, *Ad Nationes*, 13 (*The Ante-Nicene Fathers* 3:122).

In summary, Sunday was not a term used by early Christians referring to the Lord's Day. It came from paganism and had nothing to do with the Christian significance for the Lord's Day. It is apparent that Christian worship on the Lord's Day had not the slightest thing to do with pagan sun worship or adoption of pagan customs on that day. Rather, worship on the Lord's Day originated from within Christianity.

A Rest Day

A second association is the Lord's Day as a rest day from work. The first reference to the Lord's Day as a rest day was made by Tertullian in Chapter 23 of his *De Oratio* (ca. 200 C.E.). The context of his statement deals with work getting in the way of Christian worship on the Lord's Day. The statement is not meant to pronounce the Lord's Day a rest day, but a warning about Christians neglecting worship because of work.

The reference to the Lord's Day as a rest day was officially made by the famous edict of Constantine on March 3, 321 C.E. In it he declared that all except farmers should rest on the "honourable day of the Sun." Constantine's motives for declaring the Lord's Day a rest day were probably more pragmatic than theological. It seems that Christians advocating the Lord's Day as a rest day were clearly in the minority with no major influence over the Church in the fourth century C.E. There was little theological rationale given in the Church for such a move. Throughout the fourth century, the Lord's Day was not emphasized as a rest day.[4]

A Sabbath Day

A third association is the Lord's Day and the Jewish Sabbath day in obedience to the fourth commandment of the Decalogue. This emphasis came later in Christian history, culminating in the Puritan theology of the Christian Sabbath. Puritan theology said the

---

4. Bauckham, "Sabbath and Sunday," 280-287.

fourth commandment was transferred to the Christian Lord's Day by virtue of the resurrection and the New Covenant. This is called "Sabbath transfer theology." This view continues to have support.

Reaction against Puritan theology of the Sunday Sabbath arose from the Seventh Day Baptists in the seventeenth century. They recognized the error of invoking the fourth commandment in support of Sunday Sabbatarianism. Their influence would later be seen in the adoption of the seventh day Sabbath by Seventh Day Adventists in the nineteenth century. The modern seventh day Sabbatarian movement can be traced directly to reaction against Puritan Sunday Sabbatarianism. Puritan theological error provided the genesis for this reactionary movement.

There is no evidence in early church history that the Lord's Day was seen as a replacement of or substitute for the Jewish Sabbath.[5] The Lord's Day was a work day with gatherings occurring Saturday or Sunday night (Acts 20:7), moving to morning and afternoon meetings, and morning only.[6] The differing times of worship may indicate variety of worship practices rather than evolution of custom. The worship time worked around the work day.

The Lord's Day viewed in the form of the Jewish Sabbath misrepresents the meaning of the Lord's Day. Whereas the Jewish Sabbath commemorates the creation rest and Israel's deliverance from Egypt (Ex. 20:11; Deut. 5:15), the Lord's Day celebrates the new creation brought about by the resurrection of Christ. Whereas Jesus stayed in the grave during the Sabbath "resting" after his redemptive work, on the Lord's Day he arose in triumph possessing eternal life for all who believe and inaugurating a new era of salvation. The Lord's Day represents the certainty of eternal life through the resurrection of Jesus. While the Jewish Sabbath is commanded, the Lord's Day is observed because of God's action in the resurrection of Christ. The nature of the Jewish Sabbath and the Lord's Day differs in origin and theology.

---

5. Lincoln, "From Sabbath," 403; Rordorf, *Sunday*, 299.
6. Justin Martyr, *First Apology*, 67 (*The Ante-Nicene Fathers* 1:186).

The Civil Sunday

The fourth contemporary association is the secular civil Sunday. The civil Sunday is merely a secular day off from work devoid of any religious significance. It is a tradition left over from former days of religious observance. The civil Sunday is itself becoming endangered by a growing consumer society.

A Correct Understanding

What is a correct understanding of the Lord's Day from a Christian perspective? A good basis to retrieve a correct understanding of the Lord's Day begins with the resurrection of Jesus Christ. The Lord's Day gains its significance because of an event in salvation history. Several second century C.E. Christian sources indicate that the resurrection was the predominant reason for observance of the Lord's Day.

The first is an early second century C.E. text entitled *The Epistle of Barnabas* (15:6–8). In this text, the writer associates the Lord's Day with the "eighth day".

> Your present Sabbaths are not acceptable to me, but that is which I have made, when, giving rest to all things, I shall make a beginning of the eighth day, that is, a beginning of another world. Wherefore, also, we keep the eighth day with joyfulness, the day also on which Jesus rose again from the dead. And when he had manifested Himself, He ascended into the heavens.

The significance of the "eighth day" lies in its symbolism for a new creation.[7] The outstanding characteristic of this passage is the definite association between the Lord's Day, the eighth day imagery, and the resurrection of Christ. The meaning is the signaling of a new beginning in God's dealings with mankind. The Lord's Day represents "a beginning of another world" which began on the day "Jesus rose again from the dead." The result was a day which

---

7. Bauckham, "Sabbath and Sunday," 273; Jewett, *Lord's Day*, 50.

Christians kept with "joyfulness." The Lord's Day was a day of joyful assembly commemorating the resurrection. It is a day expressing thankfulness for what God has done through the resurrection of Jesus Christ which reconciled God and man. On this day death, sin, and the devil were beaten. The Lord's Day signals the time of God's triumph.

Another reference is found in Justin Martyr's *First Apology*. It gives important information of how Christians observed the Lord's Day. Two reasons are given for Christian worship on the Lord's Day. They are God's creation of light from darkness on the first day of creation and the resurrection of Jesus.[8] They signify Jesus as the light of the world who destroyed darkness and was raised triumphant. The Lord's Day was seen as a time when Christians could worship and celebrate the victory of Christ over sin, death, and spiritual darkness.

A third reference is from the *Epistle of Ignatius to the Magnesians* 9. "If, therefore, those who were brought up in the ancient order of things have come to the possession of a new hope, no longer sabbatizing but living according to the Lord's Day, on which also our life arose through him and through his death." There is some controversy because the Greek term for "day" (*hēmera*) is absent from the earliest texts. The earliest manuscript of the text actually reads "living according to the Lord's [life]." Many scholars believe that since the passage mentions "sabbatizing" (perhaps symbolizing Jewish life), then Jewish and Christian ways of life are contrasted by referring to the Sabbath and the Lord's Day. The text becomes most easily intelligible if we understand him to be symbolizing this contrast by means of a contrast of days, the Sabbath as the distinguishing characteristic of Judaism and the new Christian observance of the day of resurrection as symbolizing the new life which Christians enjoy through Christ.[9]

The Lord's Day is seen as a day commemorating and celebrating the newness of life each Christian has through the resurrection of Jesus Christ.

---

8. Justin Martyr, *First Apology*, 67 (*The Ante-Nicene Fathers* 1:186).
9. Bauckham, "Lord's Day," 229.

The Meaning of the Lord's Day

Despite other reasons given for the Lord's Day, such as "eighth day" theology and the creation of light, the dominant one throughout Christian history is the resurrection of the Lord Jesus Christ. Without the resurrection the Lord's Day would not exist. Christian history has witnessed the Lord's Day embellished with meanings alien to its origin and purpose. As a result, the Lord's Day has become misunderstood. The early church clearly understood the purpose and meaning of the Lord's Day. It is time to return to that original meaning.

First, the Lord's Day is a day of worship. The early church worshipped the One who died for them. The church habitually met to celebrate God's work through Jesus Christ. Christians partook of the Lord's Supper in commemoration of the Lord's work on the cross (see, e.g., Acts 20:7–11; Justin Martyr, *First Apology*, 67). All this occurred on the Lord's Day. Second, the Lord's Day is a day of fellowship. From the early church to the modern church, the Lord's Day has been a day for Christian meeting and greeting and giving (1 Cor 16:1–3). Christians talk together, worship together, sing together, pray together, testify together, study together, listen together, eat together, and give together. It is the day on which the church is together experiencing a little touch of heaven in their fellowship. Third, the Lord's Day is a day for hearing and studying the Word of God (cf. Acts 2:42; 20:7). Through the written Word, people can study the acts of God. Through the spoken word people can be admonished to live godly lives and disciples can be made. People can be directed to the Living Word. Fourth, the Lord's Day is the *Lord's Day* (Rev 1:10). It is not a replacement for the weekly seventh-day Sabbath, nor a day one should be required to observe.[10] It is a day exclusively claiming Jesus as the Person of that day. The New Testament does not claim the Lord's Day as holy time. It does point us to the event which did occur on that day—the resurrection. From that event early Christians derived special significance for the first day of the week. On it was fulfilled

10. Ibid., 240.

the predictions of the Lord's resurrection. The event of the resurrection created the designation of the first day as the Lord's Day—a day which Christ took possession of by his resurrection on it. It is a day for celebrating the decisive act of God in salvation history.

The Lord's Day and Society

An ever-changing society may in effect change the church's practice of Lord's Day observance. Contemporary forms of doing church are developing to cater to the whims and needs of people on the move. Whereas in the past church was practiced on Sunday mornings and nights, now the trend is to Saturday night services to augment the normal Lord's Day worship schedule. People are finding it increasingly difficult to get to church due to work schedules. The secularization of the Lord's Day has necessitated changes in how the church functions. Changes in this trend do not seem imminent.

The secularization of the Lord's Day is reflective of post-Christian America. Except for Christians who esteem the Lord's Day as important, Western civilization is moving away from a Judeo-Christian worldview to a humanistic, secular one. It may not be too drastic to claim history of Lord's Day observance is moving full circle.

The church cannot be aloof or immune to the effects of a changing society upon it. Christians must live in the world like everyone else. How should the church respond? Perhaps it can be a return to early church practice. The freedom for the church to respond to changing cultural practices is given it by the Lord's Day. It is not given by a false, contrived understanding of the Lord's Day, such as it being the Christian Sabbath. However, since rest on the Lord's Day is not prohibited in scripture, it remains every Christian's option to use it as such. On the other hand, Christians should not be criticized for seeing the Lord's Day in a non-sabbatarian sense. Church attendance should be based on worshipping the Lord on the Lord's Day, not upon some contrived invention of the church in bygone eras.

There is no formula for making the Lord's Day a holy day. The reason for this is due to the nature of the day itself. The Lord's Day is in the possessive tense, meaning it belongs to the Lord Jesus Christ. The Lord's Day is the perfect day to commemorate God's grace shown through Jesus Christ. The day commemorates the gift of salvation under the New Covenant for the believer in Jesus Christ. On the first day the Lord began a new creation through his resurrection.

Revelation 1:10 demonstrates this by the term *kyriakē* ("Lord's"), which is echoed in 1 Corinthians 11:20 where it is used respecting the Lord's Supper. As the Lord's Supper celebrates the manifestation of grace given through the sacrifice of the Lord on the cross, so the Lord's Day celebrates the time of the resurrection.

Lord's Day observance cannot be legislated or required. It cannot be subjected to legalistic rules and regulations requiring certain ways of observance. It cannot be made into what it was never intended to be. The day must be seen purely as a gift where the believer in the Lord's resurrection can freely worship on the Lord's Day. That is why no regulations were given in the New Testament to its proper observance. It originated by divine act, not divine command.

Believers should approach the Lord's Day with an attitude of gratitude. Gratitude for what God has done through Jesus Christ. Gratitude for what God is doing for believers in Jesus Christ. Gratitude for God's outpouring of the Holy Spirit on the Lord's Day so long ago. Gratitude for God's grace. The Lord's Day is a product of grace, established purely by it, not legislated to be observed unto Him. Believers are free to worship on the Lord's Day.

In order for the church to reclaim the Lord's Day, believers must come to a proper understanding of it. Understanding it as a "Christian Sabbath" will only make it more archaic. The day will not become a blessing, but another Christian duty. The day must be understood as an expression of Christian freedom in the Lord. God has provided a time to thank him by celebrating his greatest act, the resurrection of his Son.

2

THE LORD'S DAY IN POST-CHRISTIAN AMERICA

The Decline of Christendom

IT is widely accepted by many leading Christian thinkers that America and the Western world has moved into a post-Christian era. In other words, the Judeo-Christian value system acknowledged in society for centuries has been diminished and denied in society in general. Christianity is no longer the cultural force for conditioning societal values and morality.

Conversely, this certainly does not mean society in the "good ol' days" was ideally Christian with the majority of people being committed, born-again believers in the biblical sense. What is being pictured is a culture which was conditioned by its Christian heritage to find certain behaviors unacceptable and illegitimate. There was a cultural pressure to conform to accepted ways of life because society frowned on certain types of behavior. This was done not because everyone was a committed Christian, but because the majority of the population respected and valued Christian principles irrespective of whether they were truly converted Christians. It was in part because many people were not committed Christians that society later began to blatantly disrespect Christian moral standards.

Society exemplifies this trend in almost every area of life. The entertainment industry at one time had very strict standards of conduct which effectively censored foul language and explicit scenes from radio, movies, and television. Today, talk radio discusses any and every issue, television shows portraying immoral actions accompanied by explicit language, and movies which cannot develop plotlines and scripts absent the foul language and violent/sexual scenes. Indeed, the culture of entertainment perhaps best exemplifies the downward spiral of Christian influence on society.

With the void created by the absence of Christian cultural norms in society comes the influences of secularism, humanism, and rationalism to fill in the gap. These three cultural molders condition people to disregard a formative ethical and spiritual standard and allow each individual to conform to their own standard. This means the former influences on societal conduct gradually cease to have the formative power they once maintained. Thus, the standard of conformity is reversed to nonconformity to established norms. However, once the move is made away from former standards of right and wrong, the former standards are made subservient to new ways of thinking. Therefore, toleration takes precedence over conformity. In American society, this translates to individual autonomy, not communal conformity. In the final analysis, American society is heading to a condition where everything is tolerated with nothing to stand up for.

Effects Upon the Church

Within the Christian Church the result has not been positive. The patterns of modernity have influenced how Christians live and view their faith and practice. Mainline Protestantism has grown increasingly liberal, both in their theology and practice. Attendant with this has been a steady decrease in membership with thousands either leaving the church or transferring to Evangelical fellowships. Evangelicalism has not escaped the clutches of modernity. Increasingly, Evangelical churches reflect societal values rather than transform them. This is seen in their individualized expressions of faith and the harnessing of marketing concepts to grow churches. Too often personalities are followed instead of the message. The popular culture is mirrored in how worship takes place and success is measured in size and numbers. Ministry is often judged by how practical it is to people's lives in meeting "felt needs."

Theologically, the historic tenets of Evangelicalism are being challenged or made subservient to new concepts and approaches, if not outright heresies. The average Evangelical lay person does not know the basic doctrines of the Christian faith which affords pseudo-Christian cults the opportunity to deceive people for lack of knowledge. The vast majority of converts to these cults grew up within the influence of orthodox Christian churches irrespective of denomination. Indeed, the Evangelical church continues to struggle in certain sectors of its broad constituency.

The Lord's Day: A Barometer of Decline?

It has been stated by more than one Christian thinker that as the Lord's Day goes so goes Christianity. Mentioned earlier were three misconceptions of the Lord's Day which need rethinking. Following will be discussion of how post-Christian America has influenced the Lord's Day.

The secularization of Sunday has affected the Lord's Day. In past generations, the Lord's Day was a day of little secular activity which included sports, entertainment, shopping, and work. Church and family life had been the normal center of activity for a variety of reasons. Regardless of how legitimate the reasons were, the Lord's Day was culturally centered on church and family. This did not mean most people were genuine believers, but it did mean there was a cultural expectation and precedent for such behavior. The result of the secularization of Sunday is the "Civil Sunday." As a result of the culture becoming more secular, the Lord's Day has lost much of its religious emphasis and significance to the larger population. Sunday is a day to stay home and relax. The "Civil Sunday" is itself becoming an endangered species in certain areas of Western society. It is becoming more like any day of the week, consumed as it is by shopping or working.

The Lord's Day has always been the day that Christians worship the Lord and fellowship with each other. However, the increasing mentality of "what-can-you-do-for-me" and the attitude of convenience seriously compromise the biblical standard of Lord's Day worship. In other words, the purpose of the Lord's Day is being imposed upon by the culture. Sunday has become an entertainment day. Several years ago, I was reading a devotional book on the Ten Commandments written by a well-known pastor. I was particularly interested in his treatment of the Sabbath commandment. He described coming home after preaching Sunday morning to read the newspaper and watch his favorite professional football team play on television. While there is nothing wrong with watching a football game on Sunday, I was still impressed with how he could mention preaching and watching sports in the same breath. This example illustrates the forces competing for people's attention on the Lord's Day.

The creation of a "Civil Sunday" has created a void which must be filled. Since people no longer see Sunday primarily as the day to attend church and it is typically a day off from work, the void created by this has been filled by a variety of alternatives. Professional sports monopolize the television sets of millions of Americans every Sunday. Shopping malls, which are now open before noon, beckon people to come. Afternoon recreation activities also consume time that used to be for church attendance. Finally, simply staying home is now popular. The Lord's Day is in many ways the primary sports day of the week. Sundays are no longer monopolized with church activities for most people. The gulf has been bridged by secular alternatives.

Rethinking the Lord's Day in a Post Christian Church

Christians can begin to reclaim the meaning of the Lord's Day in a post-Christian America by identifying the distinctly Christian meanings for the day. To do this will require God's people making the Lord's Day a priority in their lives and rethinking a few things about the Lord's Day.

First, Christians must understand the Lord's Day is not the equivalent to the Jewish Sabbath. Often the propaganda coming from Christians who observe the Jewish Sabbath lambastes the Lord's Day as a "counterfeit Sabbath" and those observing it as "Sunday-keepers." Such titles and misrepresentations can easily be defeated if Christians understood the true meaning of the Lord's Day. The earliest Christians did not observe the Lord's Day as a Sabbath day. Rather, the Lord's Day was a day when Christians gave, had fellowship, and worshipped the Lord (Acts 20:7–11; 1 Cor 16:1–3). It was a day for commemorating the resurrection of the Lord (Rev 1:10, 18). It was a distinctly *Christian* day of worship.

Second, Christians must understand the Lord's Day is more than merely another day of the week. While the Lord's Day is not "holy" in the sense of the Jewish Sabbath (Ex. 20:8–11), it nevertheless is the *Lord's Day*. In Revelation 1:10 a term is used that literally means "a day belonging to the Lord." Additionally, the term carries "imperial" overtones, making "Lord's Day" a special designation befitting what occurred on that day—the resurrection of the Lord in triumph over death and sin.

Third, Christians must understand that the Lord's Day is more than a day off from work and a day to attend church. American people have grown up customarily having Sundays off from work. This expectation has developed into the "Civil Sunday" where Sunday is a day off from work devoid of religious significance. Many Christians have taken the Lord's Day for granted because society has customarily taken Sunday off from work, thereby making it easier for Christians to do likewise. As a result, attending church was possible for Christians because they were off work Sunday morning.

The Lord's Day is more than a rest day and a church day. It is a special day which provides the reason for Christians to rest and worship. While rest is not the essence of the Lord's Day, the Christian who doesn't have to work is afforded the opportunity of reflecting on the meaning of the Lord's Day. Similarly, attendance at church provides the opportunity to both reflect and celebrate the resurrection of Jesus. In other words, one does not have to worship and rest on the Lord's Day, one can worship and rest on the Lord's Day because they want to. Additionally, one does not have to rest on the Lord's Day to realize the blessing of the day itself. Rather, the blessing of the day results from remembering and celebrating what God accomplished on that day. Therefore, Christians should not take for granted their church attendance and relaxation on the Lord's Day. Indeed, Christians should solemnly and excitedly reflect on the day because it is the Lord's Day by virtue of his resurrection.

Reclaiming the Lord's Day

Environment in large part determines the mode of Lord's Day observance. This has proven consistently true throughout Christian history. It is this fact which reveals the central strength of the Lord's Day. The ability of the Lord's Day to adapt to varying historical situations testifies to its strength and durability. Historically, worship occurred during the night (Acts 20:7–11), during the early morning and late in the afternoon (Pliny, *Letter to Trajan*, ca. 110 C.E.), during the very early morning hours (Justin Martyr, *First Apology* 67, ca. 150 C.E.), and as a rest day (Constantine, *Edict*, ca. 321 C.E.). The variety in worship times reveals the quality of the Lord's Day as adaptable to changing situations and theologies. The reason for this adaptability is seen in the original intention for the Lord's Day given in the New Testament. It was observed as a time for worship, fellowship, and stewardship, not as a day of rest during the apostolic era. One is free to observe the Lord's Day for rest and relaxation, yet there is no scriptural command to do so. The reason is the contrast between the Lord's Day and the Jewish Sabbath during that era of Christian history.

Contemporary Christian practice of Lord's Day observance is often conditioned by societal pressures and schedules. The modern church is responding to this by offering worship services beginning Saturday night extending to Sunday night. As a result, Lord's Day observance may be historically coming full circle to what it was prior to the fourth century. In other words, during early Christian history, the Lord's Day received no recognition as a Christian day of worship by the pagan society around it. Likewise, the Lord's Day is currently losing its Christian significance due to the secularization of society. This factor carries tremendous overtones for the Christian who takes the Lord's Day seriously. Christians must cease relying on the culture to dictate Lord's Day observance.

Society more often reflects a growing non-Christian and anti-Christian attitude. When Christian institutions such as the Lord's Day get swallowed up into the weekend, they lose their importance in a secular society. Christians must respond by hearkening back to their roots. Those roots describe a Lord's Day observed in a society alien to Christian values and worldview. The repaganizing of society today will result in confrontations between Christianity and society similar to those two millennia ago. The Lord's Day is for commemorating the greatest event in salvation history: the resurrection of Jesus Christ. The Lord's Day will continue to give Christians the freedom to worship God on that day in a variety of ways at different times.

Christians should learn from the early church that the Lord's Day can be observed in a variety of ways (rest or work day), yet remain the focal day of Christian worship, fellowship, and stewardship. However, such observances should be encouraged for the right reasons and on correct biblical grounds. Christians are free to observe the Lord's Day because it points to the free gift of salvation accomplished by the resurrection on that day. Christians can respond to a secular, godless society by observing the Lord's Day in its genuine biblical form by worshipping, fellowshipping, and giving according to the scriptural testimony.

3

THE LORD'S DAY AND THE JEWISH SABBATH

THE Lord's Day has had a varied history. Beginning as a day which developed alongside the Jewish Sabbath having a character of its own distinct from the Sabbath, the Lord's Day was a day of commemoration of the decisive act in salvation history, the resurrection of Jesus Christ without which there would be no salvation (1 Cor 15:12–19). This decisive beginning made the Lord's Day distinctly tailored for Christian celebration. It was a distinctly Christian day for worship, fellowship, and stewardship representing the grace shown through the resurrection of the Lord.

The day itself was not set apart by divine decree as was the Jewish Sabbath (Gen 2:2–3; Exod 20:11). It was recognized by the apostles as a day for fellowship, worship, and stewardship (Acts 20:7–11; 1 Cor 16:1–3). It was recognized by the apostle John as a day devoted to the Lord Himself (Rev 1:10). However, nowhere in the New Testament is the day itself seen as sanctified or set apart for holy use. The day itself is not holy in the sense of the Jewish Sabbath. The reason is very simple: it was never meant as a Sabbath day. The Jewish Sabbath was always designated primarily as a day of rest following God's example (Exod 20:8–11). However, the Lord's Day was not commanded based on divine example. It was designated the Lord's Day because of an event in history: the resurrection.

The Jewish Sabbath

The difference between Sabbath and Lord's Day becomes clear when the history of the Jewish Sabbath is examined. The best place to begin to understand the Sabbath is Genesis 2:2–3, the seed-plot from which the Sabbath was given birth. From merely two verses is built one of the central tenets of Judaism and one of the issues confronting the early church. Genesis 2:2–3 states, "By the seventh day God had finished the work he had been doing; so on the seventh day he rested from all his work. And God blessed the seventh day and made it holy, because on it he rested from all the work of creating that he had done." When attempting to interpret Genesis 2:2–3 one key point becomes apparent: one should pay attention to not only what is stated in the passage, but what is not mentioned. This becomes quite apparent in verses 2–3. There are two key expressions which are not mentioned at all in this passage. The first word not mentioned is the word Sabbath. The second thing not mentioned is the expression "evening and morning, the seventh day." These deletions may not seem initially important. However, they provide an essential key to understanding not only these verses but later interpretation of passages regarding the seventh day of the week.

The absence of the word Sabbath from the account of the seventh day is extremely important. Sabbath literally means "cessation" or "to rest." Therefore, when v. 2 states that God "rested" from the work He had done, the thought of the Sabbath is clearly there in the sense of ceasing from His creative activities. However, the thought of God resting or ceasing is not developed into a full-blown reference to the inclusion of the word Sabbath. The thought of Genesis 3:2–3 is that God rested on the seventh day but that it was not called by title, the Sabbath. This will come later in the biblical record. Rest and the seventh day are connected in vv. 2–3 in a relationship where the day itself was blessed because of God's ceasing from creating. The seventh day signifies an end to God's creative activity. God is seen resting, or ceasing, from all his creative work. The sequence in vs. 2–3 demonstrates a development of thought. "God finished . . . so he rested (on the seventh day) . . . (transition) . . . God blessed, made holy (the seventh day) . . . (rationale) because he rested on it." The narrative goes from "God had finished the work (by the seventh day)" to "God blessed the seventh day . . . because on it he rested from work." The seventh day is designated as a day of *divine* rest because of divine work.

Why is the word "Sabbath" not used? First, the association of rest or ceasing from work with the seventh day is made only because of a divine action of ceasing from work. Thus, resting on the seventh day only has reference to *God's* rest. Second, in Exodus 20:11, where it quotes from Genesis 2:3 ("And God blessed the *seventh day* and made it holy"), the word "Sabbath" is entered in the place of "seventh day" ("Therefore the Lord blessed the *Sabbath day* and made it holy"). This is significant because it declares why the Israelites were to "Remember the Sabbath day . . ." (Exod 20:8). The seventh day had become the Sabbath day because on it God rested from all his work. The seventh day went from being the time of God's rest (Gen 2:2–3; "on the seventh day *he rested* . . . on it *he rested*), to the seventh day as "a Sabbath *to the Lord your God*" (Exod 20:9). The seventh day was no longer only the day upon which God rested; at Sinai it became the day on which Israel was to rest because of that divine rest. The Sabbath command to Israel is a development of the original reference to God's rest on the seventh day.

The development of God's rest on the seventh day of the week to a Sabbath day of rest for Israel brings up a very important issue. It is widely claimed by seventh day Sabbatarian scholars that the Sabbath was instituted at creation as an ordinance of the Lord to be obeyed by mankind from Adam onward. There is no evidence in Genesis 2 to support this. It is often mentioned that two great institutions came out of Eden, marriage and the Sabbath. However, closer study will reveal a definite difference between the two. The story of the first marriage is mentioned in Genesis 2:18–25. First, God declares that Adam should not be left alone without someone suitable for him. The fact that God declared Adam's singleness as "not good" (2:18) emphasizes that man's life was incomplete without a mate. This is in contradistinction with God's previous declaration in Genesis 1 that all creation was good and finally "very good" at the end of creation week. Therefore, marriage is set in the framework of not only desirability but as part of the natural order of things. This means marriage completes man's purpose in existence and is, therefore, part of God's will for mankind. Marriage is God's desire and will for the future of all Adam's progeny.

The first marriage is culminated in a statement exemplifying God's desire for marriage. It is given in the form of a command. Verse 24 states, "For this cause a man shall leave his father and his mother, and shall cleave to his wife; and they shall become one flesh." In order for the union of a man and wife to be sustained and preserved, God issued a command which would continue the sanctity of the marriage relationship. In order for a family to be formed distinct from other groups of people, a break had to occur between the husband's family of origin and his family by marriage. In other words, in order for a family to be a separate unit, a husband had to be able to independently lead his family. This could not be compromised by continued ties to his mother and father. This is important because in ancient middle eastern culture, the woman was the one who separated from her parents to join her husband, whereas the man continued strong ties to his family. On the contrary, Genesis 2:14 emphatically states that a man cannot fulfill his duties and obligations to his family while directly obligated to his mother and father.

The point in the above argument is to emphasize that marriage is guaranteed by the command for the man to separate from his family. Without this command, marriage would be doomed to fail as an institution. Therefore, marriage is ordained and maintained by this command to separate. Marriage is an institution and ordinance because of this command. Can the same be said for observance of the seventh day of the week? While it is important to observe what is mentioned in Genesis 2:2–3 regarding the seventh day, it is also important to observe what is not mentioned. First of all, no intimation is given that Adam was commanded to observe the seventh day of the week as a Sabbath day of rest. The seventh day was blessed and made holy because "on it *he* (God) rested from all the work of creating that *he* had done" (v. 3). The day was blessed and sanctified (set apart for holy use) because God had rested on it. However, though it was set apart for holy use does not mean it was commanded to be used as such. Only God is seen as resting on the seventh day. On the other hand, marriage is clearly stated in terms which identify it as a custom to be followed in a certain manner. Not only is seventh-day rest not commanded in Genesis 2:2–3, but no instruction is given about proper observance of it had it been commanded in the first place.

The most that can be said about the seventh day in Genesis 2:2–3 is that it was designated as blessed and holy, not legislated to be observed as such. Contrast this with Exodus 20:11 and a development can be seen. The seventh day went from a day on which "he (God) rested" (Gen 2:2–3) to a day which Israel was to observe as "a Sabbath *to* the Lord your God" (Exod 16:23, 25; 20:10; Deut 5:14), because on it "he rested" (Exod 20:11). In short, Israel was commanded to "Remember the Sabbath day *by* keeping it holy." Why is the phrase "seventh day" used in Genesis 2 instead of "Sabbath"? To answer this question, one must again notice who is addressed as resting on the seventh day of creation week—God. The subject is God's rest, not man's rest. The seventh day is designated first and foremost as a divine day because the God of the universe, the Creator, used this day to rest from his creative work. Therefore, when attempting to understand the meaning of the seventh day for mankind, emphasis must be given to the divine qualification given to it.

When contrasting the Jewish Sabbath and the Lord's Day, one key difference is the Sabbath commemorates what God completed (at creation), while the Lord's Day celebrates God's triumph over sin, death, and the devil (at the resurrection). The Sabbath celebrates the completion of divine activity while the Lord's Day celebrates the triumph of divine activity. This is seen in comparing the Sabbath and Lord's Day during the weekend of Christ's crucifixion and resurrection. At the completion of the creation on the sixth day "the heavens and the earth, and all the host of them, were finished" (Gen. 2:1). Afterward, God "ended his work which he had done, and he rested on the seventh day" (2:2). Similarly, John records Jesus saying "It is finished" (John 19:30)! Immediately afterward, on the Preparation day for the Sabbath, Jesus is put to rest in Joseph's tomb (John 19:31, 42). He remained in the tomb throughout the Sabbath day (Luke 23:55–56).

God completed creation on the sixth day and rested on the Sabbath after his creative work was finished. Jesus completed redemption on the sixth day and rested in the tomb on the Sabbath after his redemptive work was finished. Thus, the Sabbath figures in both creation week and redemption week. However, though Jesus' Sabbath-rest came after redemption was finished (John 19:30), it was not the end. The Sabbath of redemption week came *after the crucifixion*, yet the crucifixion was not the end of the story. The salvation accomplished by the crucifixion was yet to be revealed in the resurrection. Mark's description is similar to Matthew's, "And when the Sabbath was past" (Mark 16:1). The other two Gospels begin with the first day of the week without referring to the Sabbath (Luke 24:1; John 20:1).

Matthew and Mark detail the women buying spices immediately after sundown Saturday with a visit to the tomb on Sunday morning. Perhaps Matthew and Mark intend more by the reference to the Sabbath ending or passing than mere historical detail. Perhaps through historical detail Matthew and Mark are alluding to the theological transition from Sabbath to Lord's Day. The story did not end with the end of the Sabbath. There was more to the story. The dawning of a new day was about to occur. Had the story ended on that gloomy Sabbath, salvation would not have been put in effect. God had further plans. There was no "first day of the week" after the seventh day of creation week. However, there was at the end of redemption week. There had to be. God was about to dawn a new era of salvation. The Lord's Day is about beginnings and triumphs.

The Gospel accounts of the weekend of the Lord's crucifixion and resurrection detail many events transpiring during Friday and Sunday of that weekend. However, not much is mentioned about events occurring on Saturday, the Jewish Sabbath. Events occurring on Saturday are given in Matthew 27:22-26 and Luke 23:56. The two accounts yield interesting contrasts. On Friday afternoon, the Pharisees demanded that the prisoners on the crosses have their legs broken to hurry the dying process so as not to desecrate the Sabbath (John 19:31). After Jesus' death, Joseph and Nicodemus hurriedly prepared the body for burial (John 19:38-39, 42). Both activities occur because it was the Preparation day for the Sabbath (John 19:31-42).

Following the Lord's burial, the religious authorities of Israel approached Pilate conspiring to guarantee that Jesus' body would stay in the grave (Matt 27:62). This occurred on Saturday. By contrast, the women prepared embalming spices on Friday and rested on the Sabbath "according to the commandment" (Luke 23:56). The Pharisees and scribes, the heralds of orthodoxy, transgressed the Sabbath to keep Jesus in the grave while the women obediently observed the Sabbath and would later be heralds of the resurrection (Luke 23:56; 24:1). This contrast hints at the distinction made between the Jewish Sabbath and the Lord's Day. On the Sabbath, the Jewish religious authorities sought to prohibit Jesus' predictions of his resurrection on the "third day" from coming true (Matt 27:62, 64-65). They certainly remembered his earlier declarations that he would be resurrected in three days (Matt 12:39-40; 27:63). They used the potential kidnapping of Christ's body by his disciples as the reason for insisting the tomb be sealed and a guard posted (Matt 27:64-65). They went to such measures to guarantee the disciples would not spread news of his resurrection to the people (Matt 27:64). By contrast, the women certainly spent the Sabbath in deep remorse over the death of their beloved Lord at the same time observing the day of rest (Luke 23:56).

Contrasted with the events occurring on the Sabbath are the events happening on the following Lord's Day. Rather than being a day of sadness, the Lord's Day brought great joy (Matt 28:8). Rather than being a day of rest and death, the Lord's Day was a day of resurrection (Luke 23:56; Matt 28:6-7). Rather than the Pharisees and scribes prohibiting his resurrection on the "third day" (Matt

27:64), the angel announces the resurrection on the "third day" (Luke 24:7). While the "establishment" sought to keep Jesus in the grave through human effort, both angels and nature overruled all such efforts (Matt 28:2). While men guarded a sealed tomb (Matt 27:66), an angel rolled the stone away and the guards became as dead men (Matt 28:2-4). Whereas the Pharisees feared the disciples would spread word of the resurrection to the people (Matt 27:64), news of the resurrection spread only among the disciples (Matt 28:7-9).

These contrasts between the occurrences on the Sabbath and on the Lord's Day demonstrate the differences between the two days for Christians. Whereas the Jewish Sabbath was the interlude between death and resurrection, the Lord's Day was predicted in scripture as the day for the Lord's resurrection (Matt 12:39-40; Luke 24:21). While the Sabbath is a type of salvation rest fulfilled in Christ (Heb 4:1-11), the Lord's Day is a fulfillment of Old Testament types of deliverance and resurrection (Jonah 1:17; Hos 6:2). Whereas the Sabbath is the day of God's rest (Gen 2:2-3; Exod 20:11), the Lord's Day is the day of the Lord's resurrection (Luke 24:21; cf. Rev 1:10, 18). While the Sabbath is the day commanded to be observed because of divine act (Exod 20:11), the Lord's Day is observed by choice because of divine act (there is no scriptural command to observe the Lord's Day). While the Sabbath is a sign between God and *Israel* (Ex. 31:13,17), the Lord's Day is a distinctly Christian day observed by all ethnic groups (Acts 20:7-11; 1 Cor 16:1-3, where the Lord's Day was a day for collecting funds from *Gentile* churches to help *Jewish* believers in Jerusalem). Whereas some Christians (especially Jewish) observed the Sabbath (cf. Col 2:16; Rom 14:5-6), others (mostly Gentiles) observed the Lord's Day (Acts 20:7-11; 1 Cor 16:1-3). Similarly, a comparison between Paul's Sabbath attendance in Jewish synagogues witnessing to unbelievers (Acts 13:14, 42, 44; 16:13; 17:2, 10; 18:4), and his attendance at a distinctly Christian meeting (Acts 20:7-11), displays the differing character of Sabbath and Lord's Day. The contrasts between the Sabbath and Lord's Day are apparent starting with the accounts of creation week and redemption week. The weekend of the Lord's crucifixion and resurrection provides additional contrasts. Finally, the contrasts are seen in the life of the church in Acts. Let us not confuse what God has separated.

4

WHEN WAS THE RESURRECTION OF CHRIST?

THE almost-universal belief within Christendom is the teaching that Jesus was resurrected early on the first day of the week. There is a very small minority who believe Jesus was resurrected late on the Sabbath (Saturday), the seventh day of the week, rather than early Sunday. This teaching holds that Jesus was crucified late on Wednesday and resurrected late in the evening of the seventh-day Sabbath just before sundown, the beginning of the first day of the week in the Jewish reckoning of days. This is not a commonly known interpretation but one which merits some discussion as it pertains to the issue of the time of Christ's resurrection. The objective is to analyze this teaching and demonstrate the inconsistencies of the position. Attention will be confined to the time of the resurrection, rather than crucifixion, and the arguments used to prove a Saturday resurrection.

The Saturday Resurrection Belief

The resurrection of Christ late Saturday afternoon is based upon two key texts: Matthew 12:40 and 28:1. Both texts are coupled to show the exact time Jesus was in the grave and the approximate time he was resurrected. Thus, upon examination of both texts one can arrive at the exact duration of time between the crucifixion and resurrection. Matthew 12:40 is the key text around which the

Wednesday crucifixion and Saturday resurrection theory is based. This text is unique in the Gospels. First, only here is given the phrase "three days and three nights" as describing the time Christ was in the grave. Second, this unique phrase taken from Jonah 1:17 is interpreted as referring to an exact time period of seventy-two hours. Third, this time period is seen as *the* sign of Jonah which Jesus uses to distinguish himself as the true Messiah. The extent of time Jonah was in the belly of the great fish is synonymous exactly with Jesus' time in the grave. "Thus, the plan of salvation is involved in this story. Unless Christ was in the grave the exact time specified in this record of Jonah, He was not the true Messiah."[1] Jonah is to be seen as a type of Jesus with primary emphasis given to the duration of time each was entombed.

If Matthew 12:40 refers to the exact period of time Christ was in the grave, then it is inconceivable that he could have been crucified Friday and resurrected on the first day as is traditionally taught. Seventy-two hours cannot be put into this short period of time.[2] Therefore, another alternative must be found. That alternative posits that Jesus was crucified earlier than Good Friday and resurrected earlier than the first day of the week.

To arrive at a Wednesday crucifixion date particular attention is given to Matthew 28:1 to establish when Jesus was resurrected. Once the time of his resurrection is established, seventy-two hours is counted back from that time. Hence, Wednesday is seen as the earliest the crucifixion could have occurred. It will be argued that this teaching is correct in stressing the time element of the resurrection of Christ, and that it is important. However, the time element cannot be used to overshadow the event it refers to, the resurrection itself. Second, the expression itself is not denoting *exact* time, but relative time. Third, evidence will be given for how time was understood during the first century. Fourth, the expression "three days and three nights" is not unique at the expense

---

1. *Time Element*, 5.
2. Ibid., 5-6.

of the other time expressions given in the Gospels. Finally, textual analysis of Matthew 28:1 will be given to refute a Saturday resurrection.

Strengths of the Saturday Resurrection Belief

The time element in the resurrection was important to apostolic proclamation because of the importance of the expression "on the third day" and equivalent descriptions. On this point the Saturday resurrection proponents are correct. Additionally, the emphasis on Matthew 12:39–40 as an important scripture in this regard is also commendable. However, caution should be taken not to give this one scripture interpretive control of other clear scriptures describing the duration of the Lord's entombment. Therefore, the sign of Jonah points to a two-fold fulfillment in Christ. First, the duration of time Jonah was in the belly of the great fish, signifying entombment, is important. Second, the supreme sign of Jonah was the escape from the great fish, signifying Christ's resurrection from death. It would be wrong and ill-advised to separate the two just as it is inappropriate to separate the time reference given to the resurrection in other passages in the Gospels and apostolic writings.

This, of course, is the interpretation that Matthew has elaborated in Matthew 12:40 by citing Jonah 1:17: "Jonah was in the belly of the fish three days and three nights." While the emphasis in Matthew's statement is on the correspondence of time between Jonah's stay in the belly of the fish and the sojourn of the Son of Man in the heart of the earth, and his resurrection is not actually mentioned, there can be little doubt that the resurrection of Jesus is in view.[3]

Harold Lindsell similarly comments,

> The Sadducees and Pharisees knew the Old Testament Scriptures. They understood that before Jesus, like Jonah, could emerge alive, in some analogous fashion he had to be imprisoned for three days and three nights. They

---

3. Beasley-Murray, *Jesus and the Kingdom*, 257.

could certainly perceive the beginning of this sign, the crucifixion of Jesus. Because they took seriously what Jesus had said about the sign of Jonah, they sought Pilate's permission to make the tomb secure.[4]

Matthew 12:40 is the first instance in Matthew's Gospel where Jesus declares he would rise from the dead. This declaration is made in the context of Jonah 1:17 being a "sign" to the Pharisees and Sadducees; the only sign they would receive. The sign to that generation would be the resurrection of Jesus from the grave; a sign given great import because of the meaning attached to Jonah being delivered from the great fish. Therefore, the story of Jonah held unique significance to the Jews that Jesus used as a type of his own resurrection from the dead.[5] The sign of Jonah was not only a type of Christ's resurrection event, but also relates to the duration of time he was in the grave. Matthew wishes to draw attention to this by having Jesus quote the entire verse of Jonah 1:17. The purpose of emphasizing the time element in the grave as well as the resurrection itself was to demonstrate that not only would death be defeated by the resurrection of Christ, but "that death's claim on him had a limit."[6] That limit was "three days and three nights" based on God's sovereign will. The sign given to unbelieving Israel would be the death of their Messiah and the time he would remain in the grave until resurrection. God's promises cannot be revoked by the will of man!

Clearly, Matthew's usage of Jonah 1:17 is consistent with the other references to the time period of Christ's entombment found scattered throughout Mark, Luke, and John. Matthew's usage is unique insofar as the sign of Jonah puts greater emphasis on Christ's resurrection after three days and nights. However, as will be pointed out, this scripture cannot be made the test for judging the other time reference passages in such an exact time frame. Matthew merely uses another Old Testament expression to describe Christ's resurrection "on the third day."

4. Lindsell, "After Three Days," 15.
5. Beasley-Murray, *Jesus and the Kingdom*, 256.
6. Lindsell, "After Three Days," 15.

Weaknesses of the Saturday Resurrection Belief

A major difficulty arises when one compares all of the expressions used to describe the extent of time Christ would be entombed. That difficulty lies in the differences in the expressions themselves. The descriptions vary from "three days and three nights" to "after three days" to "on the third day." The difficulty is apparent: the phrases do not describe the same period of time using exact methods of telling time. "Three days and three nights" is clearly seventy-two hours and "three days" could be considerably less than seventy-two hours. The "third day" could refer to any point in time within either of the other two expressions. However, such mathematical headaches can be avoided in this regard. The Gospels, though using different expressions, mean the same period of time by these expressions. "Matthew clearly was not troubled by the difference between "three days and three nights" and the "third day" of the kerygma (see Matt 16:21; etc.); the expressions denote the same length of time."[7] Difficulty only arises should one phrase be made the norm for the others.

Proponents of the Saturday resurrection insist that Matthew 12:40 be used as the guideline for determining how long Jesus was in the grave. All other expressions used in the Gospels are therefore taken to mean the same as Matthew 12:40, namely 72 hours. Such a method of interpretation ignores several pertinent facts. The first of these is the general rule that when the Bible describes a period of time it refers to it in relative, not exact, terms. "Then, too, Easterners are not concerned with exact time. We know that during such a great tragedy no one would be mindful of time, or even care to know the exact hour or minute of the crucifixion, but all the apostles one way or another agree that it was on Friday, after the Passover."[8] That this is the case is seen in the varied expressions themselves. Clearly, using exact methods of time, the expressions do not exactly come together. However, if one argues that all the time references (third day, after three days, in three days, three

---

7. Beasley-Murray, *Jesus and the Kingdom*, 357, fn. 167.
8. Lasma, *New Testament Light*, 146.

days and three nights) are all speaking of the same time period, then one must find a way of making them fit together.

The solution is to see them as speaking of the same relative period of time. An exact reckoning would have them all saying different things. That the Bible writers and the witnesses of the crucifixion and resurrection understood these expressions the same is beyond dispute. "'Three days and three nights' to the Jews commonly denoted 3 days, rather than three 24-hour periods, for 'three days' were regarded as passed on the third day (cf. Esth 4:16)."[9] Further evidence of this is seen in Matthew 27:63–64 where "the Jewish leaders tell Pilate that Christ had said, 'After three days I will rise again.'"[10] This demonstrates that those beyond Christ's immediate circle knew what Jesus meant by the expression "after three days."

Greater proof the Jews saw time in relative rather than exact terms is given by the Bible's usage of time determined inclusively. This means when a time reference is given, such as three days and three nights, the duration of that time is determined not as a whole but in part. Thus, a portion of a day can be said to represent the entire day. "Among the Hebrews none of the days of the week except the Sabbath was named. In the NT the weekdays have numbers (cf. Luke 24:1). Because parts of days could be counted as wholes, 'after three days' (Mark 8:31) refers to the entire period of Jesus' burial."[11] "It has to be remembered that difficulties always arise in the reckoning of days according to Jewish usage. Thus in Halachic statements part of a day is reckoned as a whole day and already in the first century A.D. we read: 'A day and a night constitute a (full day), and a part of a (Jonah) counts as a whole (day)' (jShab., 12a,15, 17; it is in this light that we are to understand Mt. 12:40)."[12]

With regard to "three days and three nights," the expression would mean a period considerably shorter than 72 hours. Scripture bears direct witness to this usage of time in several areas

9. Horton, *Matthew*, 251.
10. Bacchiocchi, *Time*, 26.
11. De Vries, "Day," 783.
12. Delling, "Day," 949-50.

(compare 1 Kgs 12:5,12 to 2 Chr 10:5,12; 2 Kgs 18:9–10; Esth 4:16; 5:1). The expression "on the third day" itself indicates that at some point on that day would be seen as entailing the entire day. Also, the expressions "*after* three days" and "*in* three days" regarding the time of the resurrection betray an imprecise measurement of time. In other words, the expression indicates that Christ would arise *at some point* on the third day.

The second major weakness of the Saturday resurrection theory is the interpretation of Matthew 28:1 as referring to a late Saturday (Sabbath) afternoon visit to the empty tomb by the women. As was noted above, much attention is given to Matthew 28:1 as indicating a Wednesday crucifixion by counting back 72 hours from the time of the resurrection on Saturday afternoon. Therefore, the resurrection would have to occur prior to that visit late Saturday, hence a Saturday resurrection. Those who hold to Matthew 28:1 referring to a Saturday resurrection interpret that passage largely based upon the King James Version which reads, "In the end of the sabbath, as it began to dawn toward the first day of the week, came Mary Magdalene and the other Mary to see the sepulchre." The stress is upon the phrase "as it began to dawn toward" which is interpreted to mean as the Sabbath day was drawing to a close (late Saturday afternoon), and the first day was about to start (at sundown Saturday night). The first day would start on Saturday night because the Jews reckoned the beginning of a day at sundown. The women are seen coming to the tomb late Sabbath afternoon. The tomb was empty, meaning the resurrection had already occurred. "Therefore, we are given to understand that the resurrection took place at the time when the first day of the week was near at hand, beginning to appear—when dusk and lengthening shadows gave promise of a new day about to begin, but BEFORE and not AFTER. It was in the end of a day and not in the beginning of one."[13] Does this interpretation stand under close scrutiny? Does Matthew 28:1 communicate something different than the other Gospels?

---

13. *Time Element*, 13.

The controversy is primarily over the language of Matthew 28:1. In the original Greek, the phrase "In the end of the sabbath, as it began to dawn toward the first day of the week" reads: *opse de sabbatōn tē epiphōskousē eis mian sabbatōn.* Two terms of extreme importance are the terms *opse* ("in the end of") and *epiphōskousē* ("began to dawn"). The term *opse* is controversial. It can mean "Late, late in the day, evening or twilight time, after."[14] The dual meaning involved allows some latitude of translation, notably "late" or "after."

A first solution to interpreting Matthew 28:1 is suggested by the broader meaning of the adverb *opse*, which is translated in the KJV as "in the end of" but in the RSV and most modern translations as "after." The two translations reflect the dual meanings of the term, namely "late" or "after."[15] To determine which meaning is the correct usage in Matthew 28:1, attention must be given to usage in early and later Greek writings. The usage of *opse* as meaning "after" is testified by several sources as derived from later Greek usage.[16] "The confusion over whether it ought to be translated as "late in" or "after" is due to the fact that Greek writers of a later period used *opse* as a preposition followed by a genitive, which took on the meaning of "after." This accounts for the attempt to translate *opse* as "after" in some Bible translations of Matt. 28:1."[17] *Opse* is used in two other texts (Mark 11:19; 13:35). The meaning in both instances clearly refers to the later portion of a day, not after the day had finished.[18] "They are approximate time references which suggest they occurred at or near sunset."[19] Does the meaning of *opse* as "late in the day, evening or twilight time"[20] in Mark 11:19 and 13:35 necessarily mean the same meaning follows in Matthew 28:1? It is believed not for the following reasons.

14. Harris, *Biblical Library*, 14:428.
15. Bacchiocchi, *Time*, 49.
16. Harris, *Biblical Library*, 14:428; Bacchiocchi, *Time*, 51-52; *Duration*, 24.
17. *Duration*, 24.
18. Harris, *Biblical Library*, 14:428; Morris, *Matthew*, 734, fn. 3.
19. *Duration*, 24.
20. Harris, *Biblical Library*, 14:428.

First, the prevalent usage of *opse* as "after" by later Greek writers strongly suggests Matthew's reference means the same. The reason is that the other two references in Mark consistently do not mean "after," whereas Matthew only uses it on this occasion. This indicates that Matthew's usage should not be conditioned by Mark's usage of *opse*. Careful interpretation would insist each passage should be judged on its own terms and then compared. There are many Greek words which have different meanings as with *opse*. Second, rather than comparing the lexical meanings of *opse* between Matthew and Mark, comparison of the resurrection accounts would be more helpful and revealing. In other words, the meaning of *opse* is revealed by comparing Matthew's and Mark's account of the time of the women's visitation to the tomb. Comparison of the two accounts reveals the answer. Matthew and Mark are the only Gospels that mentions the Sabbath in connection with the women's visitation. Matthew's reference has already been referred to. Mark's description reads, "And when the sabbath was past . . ." (16:1). Luke and John do not mention the Sabbath at all. Rather, they merely mention the women going to the tomb on the morning of the first day of the week (Luke 24:1; John 20:1).

Interestingly, Matthew does not mention the women buying spices to anoint Jesus' body, whereas Mark does. If the women visited the tomb late Sabbath afternoon, as the Saturday resurrection theory asserts, then when did the women purchase the spices? According to Mark, it was *after* the Sabbath had passed. According to the Saturday resurrection theory, it would have been Friday afternoon before the weekly Sabbath. "Friday was the . . . .day the faithful women purchased spices . . . and prepared them."[21] The problem is that Mark clearly states the women purchased the spices after the Sabbath was over, not prior to its beginning. Furthermore, Mark confirms this by timing the women's visit to the tomb "very early in the morning, the first day of the week" (16:2). Mark 16:1 describes the activity of the women prior to their visit described in Matt 28:1 and Mark 16:2. Why did they wait until the end of the Sabbath to purchase the spices? Luke 23:56 states

21. *Duration*, 27.

they had begun to prepare spices on Friday evening. Obviously, they were unable to complete the process of preparation prior to the Sabbath. Because of this they rested on the Sabbath "according to the commandment." As soon as the Sabbath had ended, they hurriedly purchased the remaining spices needed (Mark 16:1). Mark seems to imply they perhaps stayed up all night preparing the spices for it was not until the next morning "at the rising of the sun" that they went to the tomb.

The point in discussing the timing of the purchase of the spices and the visitations in Matthew and Mark is to demonstrate how a Saturday evening resurrection creates problems in reconciling the accounts. Saturday resurrection proponents argue that the traditional position of a Sunday resurrection clouds the clear meaning of Matthew 28:1.

> Many of our Christian friends ... try to make Matthew's account of the resurrection coincide with the accounts of the women's visit to the tomb reported in Mark, Luke and John ... The mistake ... is trying to identify it (Matthew's account) with the accounts of Mark, Luke, and John. Many suggest that the King James Version of Matthew's narrative of the women's visit to the tomb contradicts the account of the other three Gospel writers.[22]

The assumption made in this statement is that Matthew is talking about a different period of time (a 24-hour period), whereas the other Gospels describe another period of time (a twelve-hour period of daylight).[23] Is such an assumption warranted? Absolutely not, for the following reasons.

1. The issue is not differentiating between two different periods of time, but determining what occurred during the intervening twelve hours of darkness Saturday night.
2. Saturday resurrection proponents must assert two different time periods in order to support their position. This creates grave difficulties. It must be proven, however.

22. Ibid., 21.
23. Ibid., 21.

3. There is no contradiction between Matthew's account and the other three accounts of the same event. Rather, they merely describe aspects of the same event with one giving details another does not. This was exemplified in the discussion on Matthew 28:1 and Mark 16:1–2. One can conclude there are contradictions only if the contradictions are created.

A third reason for reading *opse* as "after" in Matthew 28:1 is that many Bible scholars believe there is a close affinity between the Gospels of Matthew and Mark.[24] As pointed out earlier, only these two Gospels refer to the Sabbath in connection with the visitation of the women to the tomb. This is one example of the close connection between them. It is widely recognized that Mark's Gospel preceded the writing of Matthew's. If this is the case, and Matthew based his Gospel on Mark's, then to state that they describe *different* occasions of the women visiting the tomb definitely creates grave difficulties. Matthew and Mark describe the *same* event while Mark gives details Matthew glosses over or omits. If this is the case, then what is occurring in Matthew 28:1 is a "shorthand" description of what Mark details more specifically. In other words, Matthew 28:1 is a summary (with omissions) of Mark 16:1–2. Comparison of the two in the KJV follows.

Matthew 28:1	Mark 16:1–2
In the end of the sabbath	And when the sabbath was past
[omitted]	[the women] bought sweet spices
As it began to dawn toward	And very early in the morning,
the first day of the week	the first day of the week
[the women] came to see the	They [the women] came unto the
Sepulcher	sepulchre at the rising of the sun

The only detail not paralleled is the purchasing of the spices. According to Mark, this occurred after the Sabbath was over. Matthew

24. Morris, *Matthew*, 1; Guelich, *Mark*, xviv.

does not account for what occurred during the intervening twelve hours from sundown Saturday to dawn on Sunday. This creates a great problem for the Saturday resurrection proponents. Clearly, the women purchased the remaining spices on the first day of the week with preparation implied during the night prior to Sunday morning, at which time they journeyed to the tomb. Why did they purchase the spices at this late time? It was due to the rate of decomposition beginning on Friday afternoon extending throughout the Sabbath day. "Accordingly, it is now Saturday after 6:00 P.M. The bazaars are open again. So Mark relates that the three women . . . purchased spices in order that without any further delay they might go to the tomb the very next morning to anoint Jesus' body. It is true that Joseph of Arimathea and Nicodemus had already wound linen bandages around the body, strewing in a mixture of myrrh and aloes. But the dead body had not yet been anointed. The living body had been anointed (Mark 14:3–9) but not the dead one. Besides, a week had gone by since the other anointing had taken place . . . They were evidently afraid that decomposition would take place if they should wait any longer."[25]

Mark affirms with Matthew that the Sabbath was over. Therefore, *opse* in this instance means *after* the Sabbath was over, not late on the Sabbath as it was drawing to a close. Second, Mark's reference to the women buying spices after the Sabbath was over verifies the women did *not* purchase all the spices needed on Friday, contrary to Saturday resurrection proponents. In fact, the ending of the Sabbath began a series of activities extending throughout the night culminating in the visit to the tomb Sunday morning. Third, Mark's reference to the purchasing of the spices contradicts the Saturday resurrection timetable. If the women visited the tomb on Saturday afternoon, how could they have anointed the body without all the necessary spices? Luke 23:56 records the women preparing spices on Friday and resting on the Sabbath. The next day they went to the tomb with the spices prepared. We now understand their ability to do so was due to purchasing the remaining spices after the Sabbath was over. Fourth, Saturday resurrectionists

25. Hendriksen, "Mark," 678.

use a few sources to support their contention that *opse* means "late" and not "after." Their conclusion is that those Bible scholars who have chosen "late" as the meaning of *opse* "have both ample authority and precedence for doing so" and that the "translation of *opse* as 'late in' has never been invalidated."[26]

While it cannot be denied that *opse* can mean "late in the day," it remains to be proven it is so in Matthew 28:1. Purely grammatical considerations are not conclusive. However, contextual and comparative study with parallel passages demonstrates that Matthew meant the same thing as the other Gospel writers. Therefore, the meaning of *opse* stands as "after" the Sabbath was ended. A very small minority of Bible scholars opt for the "late in the day" translation of *opse*, against the overwhelming number of lexical aids, commentaries, and biblical translations that take "after" as the correct translation. Therefore, there is more reason for this rendering than merely "the fact that Greek writers of a later period used *opse* as a preposition followed by a genitive."[27]

The next term, *epiphōskousē*, is also controversial. The term can mean "to dawn, break forth, draw near, shine forth."[28] It is used in Luke 23:54 clearly to mean as the Sabbath day was coming on at sundown on Friday, the day of preparation for the Sabbath. The term can denote the coming of a point in time or describe the dawning of the sun at morning. The term by itself in Matthew 28:1 sheds no light on the proper usage of the term. However, when compared to Mark 16:2, the meaning becomes more apparent. Mark distinctly describes the women visiting the tomb "very early in the morning" on Sunday. Since *epiphōskousē* can mean "to shine forth," it seems obvious the meaning in Matthew 28:1 is similar. Whether Matthew is referring to a twelve or twenty-four hour division of the day is beside the point. *Epiphōskousē* can refer to the in-breaking of a new day (24 hours) or the in-breaking of daylight (12 hours). If it is understood as referring to the beginning of a 24 hour period, then the visitation of the women in the other Gospels

26. *Duration*, 24.
27. Ibid., 24.
28. Harris, *Biblical Library*, 12:577.

would depict a second visit by largely the same women. Such is not the case for the following reasons.

First, in all four Gospel accounts Mary Magdalene is seen going to the tomb. Why would she go to the tomb twice in a twelve-hour period to do the same thing, namely, anoint the body of Jesus? She and the other Mary are seen witnessing the burial of Jesus in Matthew 27:61. This is corroborated by Luke 23:55–56, where the women are seen witnessing the burial and how the body was laid, going home to prepare burial ointments, and not returning until the first day of the week because they "rested on the Sabbath in obedience to the commandment." Clearly, the women are seen visiting the tomb one time in all four Gospels. Secondly, the events which occurred after the visit of the women to the tomb prohibit a Saturday visitation. For one, as described in Matthew 28:5–15, all of these events would have to transpire overnight if the women are visiting the tomb late Saturday afternoon: the women going to tell the disciples all that had happened, meeting Jesus on the road back, the guards going back to report to the chief priests what had happened, the elders meeting to devise a plan, and bribing the guards to report the body stolen. Nothing in the passages indicate the guards woke up the chief priests in the middle of the night to report this. Furthermore, if Jesus' body had been stolen during the day, why did the priests tell the guards to report it stolen during the night "while we (the guards) were asleep" (v. 13)? Therefore, the literal sense of describing the dawning of the sun seems to be the more accurate rendition of *epiphōskousē*.

Having briefly examined the linguistic evidence, attention must be given to comparative context. The context of Matthew 28 gives added support to the linguistic rendition of v. 1 as reading, "After the Sabbath, at dawn on the first day of the week." First, Matthew 27:62–66 details the meeting of the chief priests and Pharisees with Pilate to make sure that Christ's body would be guarded until the "third day" (v. 64). Second, this meeting occurred "The next day, the one after Preparation," that is, the Sabbath.[29] Third, the crucifixion occurred on the day of Preparation (Friday)

---

29. Kurtright, "Preparation," 32-33; Bacchiocchi, *Time*, 35-45.

because Joseph of Arimathea came to get the body on the evening of that day (27:57–58). Fourth, since this meeting occurred on Saturday, the third day would either fall on that day or the following day (Sunday). Fifth, that the third day fell on the first day, the day following the meeting, is conclusive because in Matthew 28:11–15 the guards reported to the Pharisees that the body had disappeared. The Pharisees bribed the guards to spread the story that "His disciples *came during the night* and stole him away while we were asleep" (28:13, italics added). Which night was the body supposedly stolen?

The statement of the guards was given to the Pharisees on the first day of the week, after the women visited the tomb. Thus, the "third day" which the Pharisees spoke of in 27:64 had to be the first day of the week, since the intervening night clearly spoken of by the guards was Saturday night, the beginning of the first day of the week. The Pharisees made their request on the Sabbath day for a guard to be posted until the third day because they knew that the following day would be the third day spoken of by Jesus as the time for his resurrection. Matthew clearly sequences the events from Christ's crucifixion to his resurrection. Included in this record is the timing of the resurrection itself on the first day of the week at some point during the night. This is verified by the instructions given to the guards to report Jesus' body stolen during the night of the first day of the week.

Having given the context of Matthew 28, a comparison of the Gospel accounts of the time of the visit by the women to the tomb sheds valuable light upon Matthew 28:1. Mark 16:1 clearly states the Sabbath was over when the women visited the tomb "very early on the first day of the week, just after sunrise" (v. 2). Luke details the visit occurring "very early in the morning" "on the first day of the week" (24:1). Finally, John describes the women arriving at the tomb while it was dark "early on the first day of the week" (20:1). Furthermore, on the road to Emmaus (Luke 24:13–24), the two men told Jesus the first day was the third day since all this (i.e., Christ's sentencing and crucifixion) had taken place (v. 20–21). Proponents of a Saturday resurrection argue that "the third day since all this took place" refers not to the time of Christ's death, but to the actual sealing of the tomb which they believe would have occurred on Thursday.

> This would have included all that had been done in connection with the death and burial of Jesus. The last thing that was done was the sealing of the tomb and setting of a watch. This was done the day after His death, or Thursday . . . The time to count the days after would be from the day on which the last thing was done in connection with the crucifixion, and this was that which we have just pointed out—the sealing of the tomb and the setting of the watch which occurred on Thursday.[30]

This argument is based on the faulty premise, already discussed above, that the time from the burial to the resurrection was counted exactly. Secondly, "since all this took place" clearly begins with the *trial and crucifixion* and not the burial at all. Notice the narrative of events: "The chief priests and our rulers handed him over to be sentenced to death, and they crucified him . . . And what is more, it is the third day since all this took place" (Luke 24:20–21). "And what is more" is meant to draw attention to the fulfillment of the resurrection on the third day as Christ had prophesied. Therefore, the time element in the crucifixion and resurrection is clearly laid out in these verses. Jesus was crucified on Friday and resurrected three days later, and that third day was the first day of the week.

Advocates of the Saturday resurrection point out that the Greek expression "Today is the third day" has translation problems. Specifically, the term for "Today" is absent from the best Greek manuscripts.[31] Though the term may be absent from certain manuscripts, it does appear in the Textus Receptus from which the King James is translated. The alternative translation offered by A. T. Robertson is "One is keeping this a third day," whereas Vincent phrases it as "He [Christ] is passing this day as the third."[32]

30. *Time Element*, 24-25.
31. *Duration*, 6-7.
32. Ibid., 7.

However, such translations as these and "'he [Jesus] spends this third day,' makes for a logical transition that is too awkward to be likely."[33] Therefore, though the term for "Today" is absent from certain manuscripts, nevertheless the meaning of v. 21 is best rendered "Today is the third day." This is supported by the following consideration.

The narrative of Luke extending from 23:50—24:53 mentions the "third day" three times (24:7, 21, 46). This is important because all three references occur on the first day of the week. The women are pictured visiting the tomb very early Sunday morning (24:1). They rested on the Sabbath according to the commandment (23:56). They had not had a chance to apply the embalming solutions to Christ's body because they rested on the Sabbath. They went to the tomb with the spices they had prepared (24:1). However, the tomb was empty (24:2–3). They were "greatly perplexed" because they did not expect this scene (24:4). Suddenly, two men appeared to them and reminded the women that Jesus had foretold his resurrection when he had spoken to them in Galilee (24:4–6). Christ's statements centered on his crucifixion and resurrection on the third day (24:7). At this point the women remembered what Jesus had said (24:8). They returned to the disciples and told them everything that had happened (24:9).

The reference to the "third day" is important precisely because there was no occasion for the resurrection to occur in Luke's narrative prior to the first day of the week. Twelve hours is covered from the end of 23:56 to 24:1. It goes from resting all day Sabbath to arriving at the tomb Sunday morning. There is no indication in Luke's account that the resurrection could have happened prior to the Sabbath, on the Sabbath, or at the end of the Sabbath. The resurrection *had* to have happened at some point between sundown Sabbath and the arrival of the women Sunday morning. The reference to the "third day" in Luke 24:7 is given to the women to remind them that the tomb was empty because Jesus resurrected at some point on the day they discovered it empty. "It is now the third day, so the women should have been expecting Jesus to be

---

33. Nolland, *Luke*, 1203.

alive again (Luke achieves prominence for the third day motif by repeating it in vv. 21 and 47 and by locating all the action of chap. 24 on the same day)."[34] Otherwise, it would make no sense. Therefore, the declaration of the two men on the Emmaus road (24:21) *repeats* what they had been told by the women earlier in the day (24:9–10). They understood after being told that the resurrection had occurred that day, the first day of the week. They were passing on information they now understood.

Consideration of the linguistic and contextual evidence leads to the conclusion that Jesus was resurrected at some point during the night of the first day of the week. In Matthew, the women are seen coming to the tomb early on the morning of the first day of the week as well. This is confirmed by the linguistic evidence and by comparison of the Gospel narratives. Furthermore, the order of events described after the visitation prohibit either two visitations or a Saturday afternoon visitation. Matthew reports the same order of events as the other three Gospels and is thus consistent.

Were There Two Sabbaths?

Central and absolutely necessary to the Saturday resurrection argument is the assertion that there were two Sabbaths during Passion Week. One Sabbath was distinctly a festival Passover Sabbath occurring on Thursday of that week. The other was the weekly Sabbath on Saturday. Several assertions must be made in order for this argument to hold up.

First, the term *paraskeuēn* ("preparation") refers to *both* the preparation for the weekly Sabbath and preparation for other Jewish festivals such as Passover.[35] This assertion is supported elsewhere.[36] The issue is whether *paraskeuēn* is connected to one or two Sabbaths during Passion week. Second, the assumption is made that because *paraskeuēn* can refer to festivals other than

---

34. Ibid., 1190.
35. *Duration*, 13.
36. Thiele, "κατασκευάζω," 120; Stott, "σάββατον," 408.

the weekly Sabbath, then all the references in the Gospels using *paraskeuēn* "must be understood to be a reference to the Passover Sabbath and not necessarily the weekly Sabbath."[37] Therefore, all the references to *paraskeuēn* refer to the Passover Sabbath which was not the weekly Sabbath. Third, the reference in John 19:31 to a "special Sabbath" refers to the Passover Sabbath, not the weekly Sabbath.[38] Fourth, advocates of this view deny that the reason the weekly Sabbath was "special" (John 19:31) was due to the Passover and weekly Sabbaths falling on the same day. The reason is "there is no evidence to support it."[39]

Assessment of the Positions

The assertion that all the references to *paraskeuēn* must refer to the Passover Sabbath and not the weekly Sabbath is blatantly false. There is overwhelming evidence that *paraskeuēn* consistently referred to the weekly Sabbath (Josephus, *Antiquities* 16, 163; Synesius, *Epistola* 4; *Didache* 8:1; *Martyrdom of Polycarp* 7:1). "According to Jewish usage, it was the Friday on which everything had to be prepared for the Sabbath." Christian literature refers to it as "the day of preparation for a festival or Sabbath."[40] What is more important for this discussion is the preparation was being made for the Sabbath (Matt 27:62; Mark 15:42; John 19:31). Indeed, these references regard the *same* day: the weekly Sabbath. The assertion that it refers to another Sabbath is void of proof.

Alleged proof of a distinction between two Sabbaths is given in Matthew 27:62 and Luke 23:54, 56. In Matthew 27:62, the observation is given that Matthew refers to the Passover Sabbath as "the next day, the one after Preparation Day" and that the weekly Sabbath is referred to in 28:1 regarding the women's visit to the

---

37. *Duration*, 13.
38. Ibid., 15.
39. Ibid., 15.
40. Stott, "σάββατον," 408; cf. Carson, *John*, 604.

tomb.[41] The only way the first argument holds up is if it is *assumed* that "Preparation Day" refers to the Passover Sabbath distinct from the weekly Sabbath. This assumption is foisted upon the Gospel record. Matthew clearly refers to the same Sabbath day—the weekly Sabbath. "The Preparation was the day when people prepared for the Sabbath, that is, Friday."[42]

The context of Matthew 27:62—28:1 does not allow for two Sabbaths. The "next day" of 27:62 is the "Sabbath" of 28:1 which is clearly referring to the weekly Sabbath. Of course, the identity of the "next day" in 27:62 is not given. "He speaks of the next day and calls it the day after the Preparation, but he does not say that that day was the Sabbath. Perhaps he did not wish to speak openly of the holy day in connection with the kind of activity he was about to describe."[43] There is no grammatical indication that more than one day elapsed between Matthew 27:62—28:1. The Day of Preparation in v. 62 refers to Friday with the next day being the weekly Sabbath after which the women journeyed to the tomb on Sunday.

The reference to Luke 23:54, 56 lacks evidence as well. Two Sabbath advocates argue that v. 54 does not possess the definite article before "Sabbath." This means it refers to any Sabbath, or *a* Sabbath. Secondly, v. 56 carries the definite article, meaning *the* Sabbath. Therefore, two types of Sabbaths are indicated in both verses. This argument does not stand. First, the context of 23:50-56 clearly uses *sabbaton* in the same sense. Second, the sequence of events does not allow a long time period between two Sabbaths. Third, the narrative states the day Jesus was wrapped in burial cloth (v. 53) was "the Preparation, and the Sabbath drew on" (v. 54). The women are seen observing the burial (v. 55), returning to prepare burial spices and oils, and resting on the Sabbath day (v. 56). All this occurred on Friday with the women going to the tomb on Sunday morning with the spices they had begun to prepare on Friday (24:1). From the time they observed the burial to the end of the weekly Sabbath was approximately one day. Therefore, the

---

41. *Duration*, 20.
42. Morris, *Matthew*, 730; cf. Carson, *John*, 603-4.
43. Morris, *Matthew*, 730.

differentiation of the two Sabbath references in Luke 23:54, 56 is akin to grasping at straws to make a point. In fact, the Synoptics do not support the Saturday resurrection argument read into John's Gospel.

Though accurate,[44] the assertion that there is no evidence that the Passover Sabbath ever fell on the weekly Sabbath is not the point. It did not have to fall on the weekly Sabbath to be a special Sabbath. It was a special Sabbath because it occurred *during the week of the Passover*. Therefore, "It was a *special Sabbath*, not only because it fell during the Passover Feast, but because the second paschal day, in this case falling on the Sabbath, was devoted to the very important sheaf offering.[45] Furthermore, the Sabbath was a special Sabbath because "it fell within the Passover week."[46] "It is simpler to interpret John to mean that the imminence of a doubly holy feast day increased the ordinary desire to have the bodies removed before nightfall (when the feast day would begin) and offered a motive that the Romans might respect. The danger of violating the sacrosanct Sabbath ordinance against work may also have been part of the concern."[47]

Therefore, it is concluded the references to the special Sabbath refer to the weekly Sabbath. There simply is no evidence, especially in the Synoptic Gospels, that Christ was crucified prior to another Sabbath distinct from the weekly Sabbath. The Gospel narratives clearly picture Jesus crucified on a Friday. We must conclude with Archer that there "is no contradiction whatever between John and the Synoptic Gospels as to the day on which Christ died—it was Friday."[48]

---

44. Brown, *John*, 934.
45. Carson, *John*, 622.
46. Ibid., 604.
47. Brown, *John*, 934.
48. Archer, *Bible Difficulties*, 375–6.

A Final Consideration

One final consideration regarding the time of the Lord's resurrection is the issue of tradition. From the earliest days of the Christian faith it has been the universal acknowledgement that Christ was crucified on Friday and resurrected on Sunday. The earliest records declare the resurrection of the Lord as the primary motivation for Lord's Day observance by Christians. A couple of the early sources verify that Jesus was resurrected on Sunday.

The first clear instance of this is given in the so-called *Epistle of Barnabas* (ca. 130 C.E.). "Wherefore, also, we keep the eighth day with joyfulness, the day also on which Jesus rose from the dead" (*Ante-Nicene Fathers* 1:147). The "eighth day" metaphor symbolized for the early Christians the new beginning accomplished by the resurrection of Jesus. The second source which mentions the time of the resurrection is found in Justin Martyr's *First Apology*. "But Sunday is the day . . . Jesus Christ our Saviour . . . rose from the dead . . . For he was crucified on the day before that of Saturn (Saturday); and on the day after that of Saturn, which is the day of the Sun, having appeared to His apostles and disciples, He taught them these things."[49] Clearly, in the early to middle second century, the tradition had been handed down that Jesus was resurrected on the first day of the week. The motivation for worship on Sunday was primarily based on that tradition.

There is no record that the early church believed Jesus was resurrected on the Jewish Sabbath. The tradition handed down from the apostolic era was maintained during the immediate post-apostolic church. The tradition was based upon the clear indication of the Gospel accounts that Jesus was resurrected at some point during the night of the first day of the week. The common tradition from such early times must warn anyone advocating a contrary position to carefully reconsider that idea. If the vast weight of Christian tradition throughout history supports the traditional timetable of the resurrection, then the one advocating a different

---

49. Justin Martyr, *First Apology*, 67 (*The Ante-Nicene Fathers* 1:186).

scheme must present a water-tight case. Such is not the case with the Saturday resurrection theory.

In the final analysis, both the Wednesday crucifixion and Saturday resurrection theories would not even be suggested had Matthew 12:40 not been written.[50] A doctrine originating from one verse results in the conforming of other verses to it out of context. The end product is a complex set of propositions and scenarios which make the biblical text confusing. The chief example of this, and perhaps the greatest difficulty presented by the Saturday resurrection theory, is that Matthew's account of the resurrection (28:1) comes into direct conflict with the other three Gospels. "The Gospels cannot be harmonized to make Matthew's account of the women's visit late on the Sabbath coincide with their visits on Sunday morning, as reported by the other Gospel writers."[51]

This frank admission is truly troubling. It implies that for the sake of supporting a position out of harmony with the majority of the Gospels, advocates of the Saturday resurrection are willing to sacrifice scriptural coherence without providing an explanation to fill in the gap.

The Saturday resurrection position is clear that Mark, Luke, and John cannot be used to interpret Matthew's account of the resurrection in Matthew 28:1. "The one or more visits made by the women in the accounts quoted above are not the same as the one reported by Matthew."[52] The only explanation they can offer for this is there could have been one or more visits. This simply is not supported in Mark, Luke, or John. "The mistake many of our Christian friends make . . . is trying to identify it (Matthew's account) with the accounts of Mark, Luke, and John."[53] Of course this is the case if one interprets Matthew according to the Saturday resurrection interpretation. Matthew is not describing a different visit by the women. He is describing the same visit in different terms.

---

50. Hoehner, *Chronological Aspects*, 67.
51. *Duration*, 30.
52. Ibid., 21.
53. Ibid., 21.

5

THE TIME OF THE RESURRECTION AND THE LORD'S DAY

Introduction

THE Lord's Day is referred to in the New Testament as a day for Christian worship and assemblage. Though significant evidence is given for its observance in the New Testament (Acts 20:7, 1 Cor 16:2; Rev 1:10), past studies into the origin of the Lord's Day often lack an integrative scheme for its development into a Christian day of worship. This study proposes a connection between the origins of the Lord's Day and the resurrection of Christ. This will be demonstrated by investigating two areas. The New Testament reference to the time of Christ's resurrection and its Old Testament backgrounds is important to understanding the resurrection itself. The many passages describing the time of the resurrection are not merely historical detail, but fulfillment of Old Testament themes. Furthermore, the weekend of the crucifixion and resurrection typologically confirms the importance of the resurrection on the first day of the week.

Raised on the Third Day

In the New Testament Gospels, especially the Synoptic Gospels, the resurrection of Jesus is seen as occurring "on the third day," "in three days," and "in three days and three nights." The variety of phraseology has led to some criticism of the accuracy of these terms. However, these phrases were not only part of the earliest Christian proclamation of the resurrection, but the proclamation arose from historical fact. "Jesus' resurrection 'on the third day' was an element in the earliest apostolic faith."[1] Scripture is historically accurate when it states Jesus was resurrected on the third day. Christ's resurrection on the third day is an important aspect of the resurrection event. Therefore, the resurrection on the third day should find reference in the Old Testament from which New Testament writers found fulfillment in the resurrection of Jesus Christ. "It is probable, therefore, that the resurrection of Jesus on the third day was regarded by the early community as grounded in Scripture, and . . . Jesus related OT passages to His own destiny to give a detailed picture of the future development of His course."[2] The Apostle Paul confirms this in 1 Cor 15:4 where the Lord's resurrection occurred on the "third day according to the Scriptures" (cf. Luke 24:45–46; John 2:19, 22).

The "Third Day" in the Old Testament

Numbers are prominent in the Old and New Testaments. The numbers seven, twelve, forty, and forty-two are some of the more prominent numbers used in scripture. The number three is one of the more important and prevalent numbers. "Next to the number Seven, the number most frequently used in connection with sacred matters is three."[3] Like seven, three is a number which signifies completeness, especially the beginning, middle, and end of something.[4] "Three" and "third" are used interchangeably and are applied to years and frequently to days. "Note the easy transition to the phrase 'the third day' . . . and to the fuller expression 'three

---

1. Throckmorton, "Third Day," 630.
2. Delling, "Day," 948.
3. Pope, "Number," 564.
4. Ibid.

days and three nights' (1 Sam. 30:12; Jon. 1:17)."[5] The prominence of the number three throughout the Old Testament testifies to its importance and application to later New Testament themes such as the resurrection.[6]

The Old Testament uses the number three in diverse ways and in different contexts. For example, Hosea 6:1–2 describes the resurrection of Israel from exile, a type of burial. Jonah 1:17 tells about Jonah in the belly of the fish for three days and three nights. 2 Kings 20:5 details King Hezekiah's return to health and ascent to the temple of the Lord on the third day. Exodus 19:10–11 discusses the Lord's promise to appear to His people on the third day (see also Gen 42:18; Josh 2:16; Ezra 8:32). The theme of deliverance is prominent in the many instances where three is used in the Old Testament. Generally, the expression "third day" carries redemptive overtones. The "third day" signifies something new and better. It points to a saving action on the part of God. It shows how God works in time to affect His will for His people. The fulfillment of the Old Testament themes of deliverance and redemption are seen in the resurrection of Jesus Christ. The Old Testament texts used in association with the resurrection are Jonah 1:17 and Hosea 6:2. Both texts relate directly to New Testament references to the extent of Christ's entombment.

The "Third Day" in the New Testament

When the references to the "third day," "three days," and "three days and three nights" appear in the New Testament, a new significance is given to them. "Some of them [three day references in the OT] are taken up significantly in the NT with reference to the death and resurrection of Jesus."[7] The specific phrase "on the third day" and equivalents are "invariably associated with the Resurrection."[8] Of

---

5. Hemer, "τρεις," 687.
6. Ibid., 687.
7. Hemer, "τρεις," 687.
8. Harris, *Raised Immortal*, 11-12.

the 53 times the Greek word for "third" (*tritos*) is used outside the book of Revelation, 13 of those refer to the resurrection of Jesus.[9] Furthermore, the "emphatic dating" of the resurrection on the first day of the week in the Gospels, was important for "showing the fulfillment of the third-day prediction(s)."[10]

It is universally recognized that the "three day sayings" of Christ hold a significant place in the four Gospels, especially the Synoptics.[11] Generally, the number three is displayed prominently in the Gospels relating to Christ's ministry.

> Jesus goes away and prays a third time (Matt 26:44) and finds the disciples sleeping (Mark 14:41). Only after the third servant does the owner send his son (Luke 20:12). Pilate questions the Jews three times to render their judgment legally binding (Luke 23:22). Jesus appears a third time to his disciples (John 21:14), a third time he asks Simon about his love, and a third time Simon 'repents' of his own denial (v. 17).[12]

The continuity between the Old and New Testaments for the significance of the number three and its equivalents reinforces the biblical importance of the number itself. When connected to Christ's resurrection, it appears indisputable that the third day bears divine intention as a special reference.

The Third Day and the Resurrection

In the New Testament, the third day phraseology is synonymous with the resurrection of Jesus Christ. This is especially true in the Synoptic Gospels. Mark's description of this time period is always "after three days." Matthew and Luke modify it to "on the third day." Some have argued that a qualitative distinction exists between the "third day" and "after three days" in the Gospels. The

---

9. Hemer, "τρεις," 687.
10. Lincoln, "From Sabbath," 382.
11. Feneberg "Third," 368.
12. Feneberg "Third," 370.

Gospel writers knew what they referred to by the terms. Despite the differences, "'after three days' and 'on the third day,' are not contradictory . . . but simply idiomatic, interchangeable terms, clearly a common mode of Jewish expression."[13] A comparison of parallel usages in the Synoptic Gospels reveals the common understanding of the terms.

Mark	Matthew	Luke
8:31	16:31	9:22
after three days	on the third day	on the third day
9:31	17:23	No parallel
after three days	on the third day	
10:34	20:19	18:33
after three days	on the third day	on the third day

In the Gospel of John, reference to the "third day" is mentioned once pertaining to the marriage at Cana (John 2:1). "Three days" is mentioned one time in reference to the time of the resurrection (2:19). It was at Cana that Christ performed his first miracle "on the third day" (2:1–11). Afterward, Jesus went to Jerusalem where he cleared out the money-changers from the Temple. The Jews demanded he show a "sign" to prove his authority for doing such a thing (v. 18). His response paralleled his bodily resurrection with the reconstructed Temple to take place in three days (v. 19–21). John makes an interesting parenthetical comment. The disciples, unable at the time to understand what Jesus meant, later realized that Jesus referred to his own bodily resurrection. "After he was raised from the dead, his disciples recalled what he had said. Then they believed . . . the words that Jesus had spoken" (v. 22).

The numerous usages of "after three days" and "on the third day" clearly shows a new emphasis. They were more than merely phrases describing a period of time. They pointed to a special significance heretofore not realized. Connected with the miracle of

---

13. McDowell, *Resurrection Factor*, 122.

Christ's resurrection is the timing of three days. John drew special significance to these phrases as they related to the beginning and ending of Christ's ministry on earth. The primary theme in John and the Synoptics is the "third day" associated with deliverance and miracle—redemptive tones illustrating the work of Christ for humanity. The predictions of the time of Christ's resurrection give a new perspective on the resurrection itself.

The "Third Day" and Apostolic Proclamation

The significance of the third day in the Gospels is carried over into the apostolic writings. It should be noted that the emphasis is not primarily upon the time of the resurrection as *the* decisive feature of the resurrection. "Like so many features of the Resurrection doctrine it is not essential to salvation to believe that the Resurrection occurred 'on the third day.'"[14] Nonetheless, the expression indicates the historicity of the resurrection, not merely an abstract reference.[15]

Though reference to the time of the resurrection is not mentioned at every turn, emphasis is given it in two key references: Acts 10:40 and 1 Corinthians 15:4. They mention the time of the resurrection as a central feature of the Gospel.

Acts 10:40

Acts 10 tells the story of the gospel preached to the first Gentile, Cornelius. Peter is the central figure in this proclamation. He receives a dream of clean and unclean animals symbolizing the division between Jew and Gentile (10:15, 28; cf. 34–35). The division between Jew and Gentile continues to exist, though in the proclamation of the Gospel the distinction is no longer valid. Cornelius sends for Peter after an angelic visit (vv. 30–33). Peter arrives and begins preaching the gospel to a room full of Gentiles (vv. 36–43).

---

14. Watt, "On the Third Day," 276.
15. Ibid., 276.

THE TIME OF THE RESURRECTION AND THE LORD'S DAY

Peter begins by noting that the record of Jesus was originally given to Israel. Then he makes an astonishing statement.

"*You know* what has happened throughout Judea, beginning in Galilee after the baptism that John preached—how God anointed Jesus of Nazareth with the Holy Spirit and power, and how he went around doing good and healing all who were under the power of the devil, because God was with him" (10:37–38; emphasis added). Cornelius and a good number of Gentiles knew about Jesus and his activity in Judea. News of Christ's activity in Israel had spread to outlying Gentile districts. Peter changes the emphasis by giving details known only to the small circle of men who were around Jesus during the time of his earthly ministry. "*We are witnesses* of everything he did in the country of the Jews and in Jerusalem. They killed him by hanging him on a tree, but God *raised him from the dead on the third day* and caused him to be seen. He was not seen by all the people, but by witnesses whom God had already chosen—by us who ate and drank with him *after he arose from the dead*" (10:39–41; emphasis added).

The time of the resurrection was primarily known by the disciples and a few others at the time it occurred. The inclusion of the time element is important to qualifying what the disciples had witnessed. Rumors probably had spread that the disciples had stolen the body by night (Matt 28:11–15). Acts 10:40 is a typical "kerygmatic formula" confirming the eyewitness account of Christ's death and resurrection on the third day.[16] Peter is confirming the resurrection as a "divine act" by stating when it occurred.[17] Peter was brought to Cornelius as the communicator of special revelation (Acts 10:33). "Peter was supplementing Cornelius's scanty knowledge of Jesus."[18] The time element of the resurrection served to augment the uniqueness of the gospel message which Cornelius wished to know about. The inclusion of the time of the resurrection in the gospel message served a vital function on

---

16. Polhill, *Acts*, 262.
17. Stott, *Spirit, Church, and World*, 191.
18. Marshall, *Acts*, 190.

certain occasions. In this instance the function was to confirm and authenticate the apostolic witness itself.

1 Corinthians 15:4

The second usage of the "third day" is found in 1 Corinthians 15:4. The reference is contained in the middle of the apostle Paul's recounting of the contents of one of the earliest Christian creeds (15:3–8). Paul's statement is important to understanding apostolic proclamation of the time of the resurrection. The importance lies in the antiquity of the creed. "Ulrich Wilckens asserts that this creed 'indubitably goes back to the oldest phase of all in the history of primitive Christianity.' Joachim Jeremias calls it 'the earliest tradition of all.' Concerning a more exact time, it is very popular to date this creed in the mid-30s C.E. More specifically, numerous critical theologians date it from three to eight years after Jesus' crucifixion."[19] The content of the creed reveals the original proclamation and belief of the early church. The contents were handed down from the earliest era of the church.

"The independent beliefs themselves, which later composed the formalized creed, would then date back to the actual historical events themselves. Therefore, we are dealing with material that proceeds directly from the events in question and this creed is thus crucial in our discussion of the death and resurrection of Jesus."[20] Where did Paul receive his information? By the apostle's own testimony, Jesus appeared to him last (1 Cor 15:8–9). Paul did not personally witness the contents of the creed during the life of Christ. He received the information by revelation and from the risen Lord and from those who were closest to Jesus during his life. He passed the information on to the Corinthians.

Paul seems to indicate where he obtained this information in Galatians 1:18–19. Three years after his conversion Paul went to Jerusalem to acquaint himself with Peter and stayed for fifteen

---

19. Habermas, *Verdict*, 125.
20. Ibid., 125.

days. Peter was the ideal person to relay information. He was a prominent leader in the Jerusalem church and perhaps the closest to Jesus. It seems clear that something more was involved than merely a social call. "Paul was quite ready to acknowledge his indebtedness to Peter for further information—no doubt primarily background information about the ministry of Jesus while on earth as well perhaps as the very beginnings of the new movement centered on the risen Christ."[21]

Paul went to Peter to fill in the gaps in his knowledge about the Jesus who revealed himself to him. His conversion experience revealed the gospel to him and gave him the call as the apostle to the Gentiles. His visit with Peter informed and confirmed details in his knowledge about the life of Jesus. "He used his time with Peter, the one who had been closest to Jesus, to make inquiry, to draw out the sort of information which had not come to him with the apostle-making gospel-giving revelation three years earlier."[22] Even more important is the fact that Paul's recounting of the gospel events completely coincides with the other apostolic eyewitnesses. "Paul's factual account was the same as that of the other apostles, in spite of the fact that Paul distinguished himself from the others."[23] Paul's reference to the resurrection occurring on the "third day" was part of the earliest apostolic confession of the gospel. Paul was simply passing on what he had learned.

Evidence for this is seen in Paul's reference to the third day as being "according to the scriptures" (v. 4). It is mentioned with regard to Christ's crucifixion as well. The crucifixion and resurrection are mentioned as being grounded in scripture rather than merely eyewitness accounts. Jesus' crucifixion and the time of his resurrection were predicted in the Old Testament. Jesus' third day resurrection "certainly implies a reference to Hosea 6:2."[24] The resurrection occurring on the third day is based on the historical

---

21. Dunn, *Jesus, Paul and the Law*, 112-3.
22. Ibid., 113.
23. Habermas, *Verdict*, 124.
24. Beasley-Murray, *Jesus and the Kingdom*, 246; McArthur, "On the Third Day," 82.

and verified witness of the apostles that fulfilled certain Old Testament references to the "third day." The reference to the third day in 1 Corinthians 15:4 is witnessed to idiomatically in Hosea 6:2. Though Jesus' resurrection on the third day is clearly based on the Old Testament, that realization did not dawn on the early church until after the resurrection (see Luke 24:45–46). In John 2:21–22, a parenthetical note is inserted in Christ's statement paralleling his body with the temple being raised up in three days. The meaning was not understood until "after he was raised from the dead" when "his disciples recalled what he had said." Christ's statement about being raised "in three days" was based on the scriptures, not merely on what he said (v. 22).

Paul's recounting of the resurrection occurring on the third day indicates it played an integral role in early apostolic belief about the resurrection of Christ. To maintain they emphasized the resurrection alone is insufficient. The time element is clearly stated as being a central motif in the proclamation of the resurrection event. Christ's resurrection on the third day according to scripture strongly indicates the time of the resurrection was important in apostolic proclamation.

The "Third Day" in the Earliest Christian Creeds

The central role played by the expression "third day" in earliest Christian tradition is also displayed in the formulation of the earliest post-apostolic creeds. As stated earlier, 1 Corinthians 15:4 can correctly be called a model Christian creed going back to the very beginnings of the church. Subsequently, formulations of second to fourth century creeds bears witness to the Corinthian creed being a model for their formulation. This is seen in their similar content. For example, the so-called "Apostles Creed" bears direct witness to this similarity. This creed is the earliest known post-apostolic creed whose origin is clouded. It reads,

> I believe in God the Father Almighty, Maker of heaven and earth: And in Jesus Christ his only Son our Lord: Who was conceived by the Holy Ghost, Born of the

> Virgin Mary: Suffered under Pontius Pilate, Was crucified, dead, and buried: He descended into hell: The third day he rose again from the dead: He ascended into heaven, and sitteth on the right hand of God the Father Almighty: From thence he shall come to judge the quick and the dead.

Note should be taken of the similarity at the core of both the Corinthian and Apostle's Creeds. They both mention directly that Jesus died, was buried, and was raised from the dead on the third day. In second century Christian apologetic literature, emphasis was also placed on the third day as a defining expression. Justin Martyr, the first true Christian apologist, in his *Dialogue with Trypho*, describes the historical fact of the resurrection by associating it with the time it occurred: "For indeed the Lord remained upon the tree almost until evening, and they buried Him at eventide; then on the third day He rose again."[25] Though not every creed of the Patristic era contained such phraseology, it still remains impressive that the original proclamation of the resurrection occurring on the third day remained a standard formula to such a late date. Furthermore, it seems safe to conclude such an emphasis was intended from the beginning due to its grounding in scripture. Therefore, even into the first two hundred years after the apostolic era, the time element of the resurrection remained vital to the recounting of the resurrection.

The Importance of the Time of the Resurrection

The time of the resurrection of Christ on the third day as grounded in scripture is an important aspect of the resurrection and its proclamation. The evidence in the Old and New Testaments leads to this conclusion. Also apparent is its importance in the verification of the resurrection itself. It stands as a sign of God's vindication of His Son and the deliverance of mankind from the sting of eternal death. Christ's resurrection on the third day continues the Old

---

25. Justin Martyr, *Dialogue with Trypho*, 97 (*The Ante-Nicene Fathers* 1:247).

Testament emphasis on the third day as a time of deliverance. The supreme fulfillment and illustration of this is the resurrection on the third day according to scripture. This reality carried over into the post-apostolic creeds as a description of the resurrection.

The "Third Day" Becomes the Lord's Day

In this section attempt will be made to link the significance of the resurrection on the third day with events during the weekend of Christ's crucifixion and resurrection. The primary goal is to demonstrate the linkage between the "third day" predictions for Christ's resurrection and their fulfillment on the first day of the week. This will be done by discussing the typological significance of events occurring during the weekend of Christ's crucifixion and resurrection.

The chronology of events introduces the typological importance of the events which transpired during the time of Christ's death and resurrection. Jesus is seen in all the Gospels as being crucified on Friday morning with his death in the afternoon (Matt 27:45–46; Mark 15:33–34; Luke 23:44–46; John 19:31).[26] Coinciding with Jesus final cry, the temple curtain separating the Holy from the Most Holy Place was torn from top to bottom (Matt 27:51; Mark 15:38; Luke 23:45). All the Gospels set the time of the resurrection on the first day of the week (Matt 28:1; Mark 16:1; Luke 24:1; John 20:1). Significant in this chronology is that on the first day of the week after Passover, the initial offering of grain was given which began the countdown to Pentecost 50 days later (Lev 23:15–16).[27]

Jesus as the Lamb of God sacrificed during Passover week is typologically recognized in other parts of scripture (1 Cor 5:7; Heb. 10:1–18; Rev 5:6–14; 7:14), with his crucifixion happening at the time the Passover lambs were being slain.[28] Jesus as the High

---

26. Hoehner, *Chronological Aspects*, 74.
27. Ibid., 74.
28. Ibid., 76, 92.

Priest of Passover week is also testified to (Heb 8:1–6; 9:11–14). Jesus as the once for all Passover sacrifice tearing open the veil and thereby opening the way directly to God is emphasized (Heb. 9:12; 10:12,19). Finally, Jesus as the "first-fruits" of the harvest is given typological significance (1 Cor 15:20, 23).

Christ's death and resurrection thus fulfilled the significance of the Passover weekend. The resurrection on the third day encompassed all the foregoing events from crucifixion/sacrifice to resurrection/firstfruit offering. Emphasis will now be given to demonstrating the association of Christ as the firstfruits of the resurrection (harvest) with the significance of the third day ending on the first day of the week. The association of Christ with the firstfruits of the harvest is recognized primarily in 1 Corinthians 15. Pentecost was the festival of the harvest of grain which occurred fifty days after the first offering of barley was given on the first day of the week after the Passover Sabbath. "In the Old Testament the firstfruits were the initial act of the annual production of grain, wine, oil and sheared wool that was offered to God in acknowledgment of his ownership of all the produce of the field and flocks and in thanksgiving for his generous provision (Exod. 23.16, 19; Lev. 23.10; Num. 18.8, 12; Deut. 18.4; 26:2,10; 2 Chr. 31.5; Neh. 10.37)."[29]

Paul draws typological significance to this in 1 Corinthians 15:20–23 in association with the resurrection. Paul argues that Christ's resurrection from the dead is a demonstration and guarantee of the final resurrection of all believers from the dead. Hence, by his resurrection, Jesus is the "firstfruits" of the resurrection of all believers when the end comes (v. 23). This is similar to Paul's declaration in Colossians 1:18 that Jesus is the "firstborn from among the dead." Paul is stating that the offering of the first grain on the day after the Passover Sabbath is a type of the resurrection of believers at the end of time. Therefore, the offering on the first day after Passover Sabbath is connected with Christ's resurrection on the first day after Passover Sabbath.

---

29. Harris, *Raised Immortal*, 110.

The connection of Christ as the firstfruits of the resurrection with Christ's proclaimed resurrection on the third day is found in 1 Corinthians 15:4. That this text is important is attested by its derivation from scripture itself. The Old Testament significance to the third day as a day of deliverance and resurrection applies to the first day, for on that day Jesus was raised from the dead. Jesus as the firstfruits of the final resurrection of believers occurred on the first day of the week, the time for the firstfruits to be given. There exists a relationship between the time element for Christ's resurrection (on the third day) and the day on which it occurred (the first day of the week, the day of the firstfruits).

Paul is attempting to relate the earliest Christian proclamation of the resurrected Christ on the third day (15:4) with the resurrection of believers on the final day (15:23) by drawing attention to Christ's resurrection which occurred on the first day of the week, the day of the firstfruit offering (15:20). "At this point we might note that the experience of Christ in rising from the grave on the 'third day' makes him distinct from believers who . . . rise from the dead on the 'last day'. He is the firstfruits of the resurrection harvest, unique in both his status and his experience with regard to resurrection."[30] Thus, there is a linkage between Christ's resurrection on the third day with Jesus as the firstfruits of the resurrection on the first day.

The significance of Pentecost enlightens the importance of the resurrection on the third day occurring on the first day of the week. The first offering on the first day after Passover Sabbath was merely the beginning of the harvest with the final celebration occurring at Pentecost fifty days later, again on the first day of the week. It is important to view both as ends to one harvest. "The firstfruits are related to the harvest as the part is to the whole."[31] The point is that the resurrection of Christ guarantees the final resurrection of all believers on the last day. On the third day, Christ was the "first to rise from the dead" (Acts 26:23) on the first day of the week. Without his resurrection on the first day, there could be

30. Ibid., 43-44.
31. Ibid., 110.

no resurrection on the final day (1 Cor 15:15–16). For prior to the "third day," the term "the resurrection" "could have no reference except to the 'last days' . . . It was what happened 'on the third day,' and the eschatological significance attached to it, that alone could make men think of applying the term 'the resurrection,' to a point within history."[32]

Therefore, the third day was a day of redemption and salvation. "The third day is the day salvation commences."[33] Christ's resurrection on the third day marked the "advent of the End, or at least its beginning."[34] The firstfruits symbolize the union of Christ's resurrection and the resurrection of believers into one. Only the resurrection of Christ, the first man raised from the dead, can put in effect resurrection for believers. "Paul cannot envisage the firstfruits without the full harvest, nor can he contemplate the full harvest without the firstfruits."[35]

The timing of the Lord's resurrection is indelibly linked with the resurrection event itself. Contained in one of the early creeds of Christendom is that Jesus was raised on the third day (1 Cor 15:4). This was scripturally mandated and predicted (Luke 24:45–46; John 2:19, 22; 1 Cor 15:4). The prediction of resurrection on the third day was fulfilled during Passover weekend. The third day prediction was fulfilled on the first day of the week paralleling the offering of the firstfruit of the harvest (1 Cor 15:20, 23). The parallel between Christ's resurrection on the first day and the firstfruit offered on the first day connects the time of the resurrection to the resurrection of the dead on the final day. Evidence for this lies in the fact that whereas the resurrection was always associated with the "third day", the appearances of the risen Christ always are associated with the first day of the week (compare Luke 24:7, 21, 46 with John 20:19, 26).[36]

---

32. Robinson, "Resurrection," 44.
33. Feneberg "Third," 370.
34. Harris, *Raised Immortal*, 95.
35. Ibid., 111.
36. Ibid., 111–12, 39–40.

The significance of Pentecost is the outpouring of the Holy Spirit upon all humanity, signaling the harvest of the Lord which is to continue to the final day. The first day of the week is prominent because on that day Christ was resurrected, inaugurating the last days, and Pentecost may have occurred, inaugurating the harvest of the Holy Spirit during the last days (see Acts 2:16–20). Christ was crucified and resurrected over Passover weekend to typologically fulfill the third day predictions on the first day of the week. The objective was to establish the Old Testament fulfillment of the third day references in the Passover celebration, culminating in the resurrection of the Lord on the first day of the week. Christ's resurrection on the first day was important for on that day was fulfilled the scriptural predictions of Christ's resurrection from the dead on the third day. The first day of the week is a memorial of both Christ's resurrection and the coming day of resurrection for all believers. It is a day of both retrospection and anticipation. The resurrection of Christ on the first day guarantees the resurrection of believers on the last day. Therefore, each Lord's Day is an occasion to celebrate both the work of Christ at the resurrection and the future resurrection of all believers. It is a day which joins the past with the future.

Conclusions

The resurrection and the time of the resurrection were founded upon the Old Testament. They did not occur in isolation independent of biblical foundation. Indeed, the overwhelming evidence verifies that both occurred "according to the scriptures" (1 Cor 15:4). The origin of the Lord's Day resulted from the fulfillment of the resurrection on the third day "according to scripture." It would be incorrect to assert the Lord's Day was directly predicted in the Old Testament. However, the time on which it occurred definitely was predicted. The time of the resurrection is important in understanding the resurrection itself. Christ's resurrection fulfilled the Old Testament types of "firstfruit" offerings immediately after the Passover. The events occurring on the weekend of Christ's death, burial, and resurrection demonstrated the typological significance of Old Testament festivals and events. The Lord's Day was the day on which the fulfillment of the Old Testament types regarding the resurrection occurred.

6

THE LORD'S DAY IN THE ACTS OF THE APOSTLES

ACTS 20:7–12 is the first clear, unambiguous reference to a gathering of Christian believers on the first day of the week.[1] The account details a portion of Paul's trip to Jerusalem during his third missionary journey (Acts 18:23—21:17; 53–57 C.E.). While on his journey to Jerusalem he stopped in Troas for a period of seven days (20:6). While there he joined in on a meeting of believers the night before his departure the following day. Several key questions arise regarding this meeting. Was the meeting a regular or unique gathering of the church at Troas? When on the first day did the meeting occur, Saturday night or Sunday? What was the purpose for the inclusion of the event in Luke's account of Paul's journey?

The Meeting: Regular or Unique?

Was the meeting at Troas a regular occasion in which Paul simply attended the day prior to departure, or is it a spontaneous gathering to bid farewell to Paul? Some believe it was a special meeting in every respect. "There is no evidence that this gathering was a regular weekend service, as it is often assumed to have been."[2]

---

1. Longenecker, "Acts," 509; Lenski, *Acts*, 825; Specht, "Sunday in the New Testament," 122.

2. Specht, "Sunday in the New Testament," 122; see Lenski, *Acts*, 825.

Others favor a farewell gathering as being the reason for the meeting.[3] Believing that the meeting was occasioned by Paul's departure the following day misses one important factor. "The text does not say that because Paul wished to continue his journey the next day, therefore they assembled on the first day of the week. Rather it plainly says that the brethren were gathered on the first day of the week to break bread, and Paul, because he planned to leave the next day, prolonged his discourse into the wee hours of the morning."[4]

The rationale for holding the meeting was not because of Paul's departure, but because they "came together to break bread" (20:7). Paul attended this meeting in order to speak to those assembled. Paul spoke until midnight because he was leaving the next day (v. 7). The passage does not say, "Because Paul wanted to go away on the next day, we assembled on Sunday in order to break bread."[5]

> It is, therefore, not satisfactory to interpret the situation the other way round by supposing that the assembly was held on Sunday as an exception because Paul wished to depart on the following day. The exceptional element was not the assembly on Sunday (that was, in fact, the usual practice), but only the fact that Paul prolonged his address until midnight on account of his impending departure.[6]

The length of the meeting was conditioned by the time of departure. The meeting itself was not conditioned by Paul's departure. This is evidence from the text that the meeting was not unique. The gathering of believers on this occasion probably indicates a custom of regular meetings by the believers at Troas. Paul joined this meeting of believers during their regular meeting in order to speak to them before he left.

---

3. Bacchiocchi, *Sabbath to Sunday*, 107.
4. Jewett, *Lord's Day*, 61.
5. Rordorf, *Sunday*, 200.
6. Ibid., 199-200.

The length of Paul's visit in Troas is evidence that the meeting was regular. Verse 6 states that Paul stayed in Philippi for the Feast of Unleavened Bread. Afterward, he journeyed five days until his arrival in Troas to join up with those who went ahead of him (v. 5). Paul and his party stayed in Troas for a full week ("seven days," v. 6). Why would Paul and his party stay in Troas for seven days? Paul immediately left the meeting of believers as soon as he was finished speaking the next morning (v. 11). His departure seemed to be conditioned by the time of the meeting (v. 7, "On the first day of the week . . . Paul spoke to the people"). This indicates that Paul waited a full week for an opportunity to speak with the assemblage of believers on the first day of the week. No indication is given in v. 6 regarding the reason Paul stayed in Troas for seven days. Immediately following this notation is record of the meeting occurring just before Paul's departure on the seventh day of his stay. Perhaps Paul arrived too late the previous week to speak to the assembled believers, or perhaps he was awaiting the departure of his ship.[7] Whatever the case, Paul seems to have waited a full week to speak to the assembled believers.

The meeting at Troas displays the standard biblical descriptions of worship, fellowship, and hearing the word of God during a gathering of God's people. The gathering was called for the "breaking of bread" (*klasei tou artou*). This phrase is used as a description of a fellowship meal and the Lord's Supper (cf. Acts 2:42, 46). Acts 2:42 refers to the early church as enjoying the "breaking of bread" (*klasei tou artou*) as part of their worship and fellowship with one another. In 1 Corinthians 10:16, the breaking of the bread is a phrase describing the bread of the Lord's Supper. "That the Lord's Supper was accompanied by a larger fellowship meal may be indicated by the reference to their 'eating' in v. 11 (cf. 1 Cor 11:20ff)."[8] Furthermore, Luke would understand it as the "Lord's Supper in the context of a fellowship meal, as in the upper room in Jerusalem" (see Luke 22:20; 24:30–35).[9]

---

7. Polhill, *Acts*, 418.
8. Ibid., 418.
9. Stott, *Spirit, Church, and World*, 319.

Another indication of this gathering in Troas as a description of a Christian worship service is gained by comparing Acts 2:42 with 20:7. Acts 2:42 pictures the believers gathering together (vs. 44, 46) for eating and fellowship. Acts 20:7 pictures believers coming together to break bread. The location of the meetings occurs in the homes of believers, a location commonly used for Christian worship services. Believers in Jerusalem are pictured as devoted to the teaching of the apostles. Believers in Troas are pictured as listening to the apostle Paul's teachings. By all indications, the meeting in Troas was a typical Christian gathering for fellowship and worship; not an atypical event in Luke's account of occurrences during Paul's third missionary journey.

Those advocating the occasioning of the meeting as being for a unique purpose (Paul's departure) are not totally incorrect. The uniqueness lies not in the time of the meeting, but in the fact that it is the only place in the book of Acts where Paul is seen addressing believers on an explicitly mentioned day, the first day of the week. In the instances where he is seen addressing Jews and God-fearers in the synagogue on the Sabbath, the reason is primarily to preach the gospel to unbelievers in an assembled audience (Acts 13:14, 42, 44; 16:13; 17:2 ["As was his custom"]; 17:10; 18:4).

The Time of the Meeting

There is some controversy about when on the first day of the week the meeting at Troas occurred.[10] Most interpreters believe that the meeting occurred on a Sunday evening and lasted overnight into Monday morning.[11] This view is based upon the Roman reckoning of a day from midnight to midnight. If Luke used the Roman calculation, the meeting would have occurred on Sunday night since that would have been the evening of the first day of the week. Other scholars believe the meeting occurred on a Saturday night using the Jewish reckoning of sundown to sundown. "From the

---

10. Conzelmann, *Acts*, 169.
11. Stott, *Spirit, Church, and World*, 319.

context it appears that it was in the evening, perhaps late, for the apostle prolonged his sermon until midnight ... The form of the expression suggests that it was the evening after the Sabbath, not the evening after the day following the Sabbath."[12]

In Acts 20:7, the Greek term used for "the next day" is *epaurion*. This word is used several times in the book of Acts. If it here refers to a portion of the same day, Paul would have left during the daylight period of the first day of the week (the Jewish method). If it refers to a separate day altogether, Paul would have left during the next 24-hour period (the Roman method). Since Luke was a Gentile writer it is assumed the Roman method was used.[13] However, "the next day" could merely refer to the next daylight period (the following morning), not the next calendar day.[14]

Some have argued that it could not be a Saturday night meeting because there is no evidence of this custom in later Christian tradition.[15] This theory "cannot explain why the early Christians met on the evening of the first day of the week" later on.[16] It must be assumed that Christians moved from worship on Saturday night to Sunday night. Historically, worship patterns moved from evening (Acts 20:7, regardless of the day), to morning and evening on the same day (Pliny, *Letter to Trajan*; ca. 110 C.E.), and to morning only (Justin Martyr, *First Apology* 67; ca. 150 C.E.). Changes in worship patterns over time may not eliminate a Saturday night meeting in Acts 20:7. Explaining the differences in worship patterns between Pliny's and Justin's accounts also may not be necessary. All the worship times probably were occasioned around the work day, especially the accounts of Pliny and Justin. Acts 20:7 may refer to the same situation, except the work day would be Saturday.

---

12. Riesenfeld, *The Gospel Tradition*, 127-128.

13. Turner, "Sabbath, Sunday, and the Law," 130.

14. Rordorf, *Sunday*, 201.

15. Jewett, *Lord's Day*, 54; Turner, "Sabbath, Sunday, and the Law," 155, fn. 241.

16. Jewett, *Lord's Day*, 54.

An additional consideration is the theory that Jewish Christians continued to worship in the synagogue until they were driven out.

> This made the church's most natural time for the Lord's Supper Saturday evening, i.e., the beginning of Sunday, as seems to be the case in Acts 20:7. When under Trajan these evening gatherings apparently became illegal, the Supper was moved to the early Sunday morning. This move cut the last links with the Sabbath and made the connection with Christ's resurrection as a justification for specifically Sunday worship—something that must have been there from the first—virtually self-evident.[17]

Such a view postulates that the church began Lord's Day observance from within the bosom of Judaism. Such a viewpoint has merit if the Lord's Day is viewed as scripturally derived. However, this explanation does not explain fully how the practice spilled over to the Gentile church which confronted entirely different social situations. Perhaps a plausible explanation for Gentile church services on Saturday night is the time of the Lord's resurrection. Rather than being an after Sabbath activity, perhaps Saturday night services were conditioned by the work day and the time of the resurrection.

The differing times of worship may simply indicate a variety of worship practices in the early church rather than the evolution of custom. They may record the worship patterns of that particular region, not indicative of a universal custom of Lord's Day service times. Regardless of whether the meeting in Acts 20:7 was on Saturday night or Sunday, the meeting still occurred on the first day of the week. Eliminating one alternative (Saturday night) by pointing out deficient evidence linking it with later Christian custom (Sunday morning and/or night) perhaps reads more into the contrast than is warranted.

---

17. Ellison, "Sunday," 940.

The Events at the Meeting

Many scholars concentrate solely on Acts 20:7. However, it seems conclusive that more appears in this account than meets the eye. *What* occurred in this meeting must not be separated from *when* the meeting occurred. The story centers on what occurred at the meeting with the slave Eutychus. "The detail is very brief and merely sets the scene for the main action—the death and restoration of Eutychus."[18] The story connects the importance of the time of the meeting with the events going on in the meeting. The sequence of events supports a Saturday night meeting rather than a Sunday night event. The story is given as a parallel to the time of the resurrection of Christ on the first day of the week. In the story of Eutychus,

> there are some rather strong linkages with the resurrection. It was Easter time. The Passover had just ended, the season of Jesus' death and resurrection (v. 6). It was the first day of the week, the day of Jesus' resurrection (v. 7); and, given the season, Paul may well have been expounding on that event. The restoration of Eutychus's life was a vivid reminder to the Christians of Troas that the Jesus whom Paul had been preaching was indeed the resurrection and the life.[19]

The sequence of events in the story parallels the sequence of events transpiring during the night of Christ's resurrection. Eutychus is seen falling out of the third story window to his death at some point between midnight and Paul's departure the following morning (vs. 10–11). This closely parallels the Gospel accounts of the women going to Christ's tomb on Sunday morning only to find it empty. The women are pictured going to the tomb while it was still dark or as the sun was just beginning to rise (John 20:1; Mark 16:2). This indicates that Jesus was resurrected at some point during the night hours between midnight and dawn. Just as Luke does

---

18. Turner, "Sabbath, Sunday, and the Law," 129; 155, fn. 233.
19. Polhill, *Acts*, 419.

not give us the exact time of Eutychus' resurrection, so the Gospel writers do not give the exact time of Christ's resurrection.

Another parallel is Paul's reply to the crowd's reaction. Upon resurrecting Eutychus, the first exclamation from Paul was "Don't be alarmed... He's alive" (v.10)! One of the first statements of the angel at Christ's tomb was "Don't be afraid... He is risen" (Matt 28:5-6), and "Don't be alarmed... He has risen" (Mark 16:3)! The words of Paul "comforted" the crowd of Troas believers (v. 12). "It was more than comfort. They were encouraged and strengthened in their faith by what they had witnessed that night."[20] No less could be said of the angel's remarks to those addressed at Christ's tomb. The account of the meeting at Troas suggests a parallel between the timing of Eutychus' resurrection and Christ's resurrection. Both events are seen as occurring on the first day of the week. A connection is drawn between the resurrection of Jesus on the first day of the week and the Christian meeting occurring at Troas on the first day of the week. What is pictured in Acts 20:7-12 is the first day being a day for Christian worship, fellowship, and proclaiming of the word.

The theme of resurrection, so apparent in the account, illustrates a possible connection between the time of Christ's resurrection and the time of Christian worship. Acts 20:7-11 pictures the early church worshiping the Lord on the first day of the week. There is some indication that Luke included the story of Eutychus to link the time of the resurrection of Christ, the time of the resurrection of Eutychus, and Christian worship to demonstrate the rationale for Christian worship on the first day of the week. If this is the case, then Acts 20:7-11 is a strong indication of the importance of Christian worship on the Lord's Day.

---

20. Ibid., 420.

7

THE LORD'S DAY
AND CHRISTIAN STEWARDSHIP

THE Lord's Day stands for many different things. The primary significance of the Lord's Day is as a reminder of God's grace. The grace of God was supremely and manifestly expressed in the life, death, and resurrection of Jesus Christ. The community founded by grace was the church, the *ekklēsia*. As such the church was to manifest and extend the character and grace of God to the world. During his third missionary journey, the apostle Paul dedicated a significant portion of his time and attention to one expression of grace shown by the church. The "collection" was a major effort on the part of Paul to encourage the church to express grace across cultural boundaries, from Gentile churches to the struggling Jewish church in Jerusalem.

Paul devotes considerable attention to the collection for Jerusalem in his epistles to the church at Corinth (1 Cor 16:1–4; 2 Cor 8–9). The reference in 1 Corinthians 16:1–4 mentions the first day of the week. There are several aspects in this account which stand out. Paul detailed a plan for collecting the money for "the saints" in Jerusalem. He had advised the Galatian churches to follow the same plan. The plan called for each individual (or family) to set aside a relative amount of money each week on the first day, either privately or corporately at church. Paul would come by on his journey to collect the accumulated sum so no contributions would have to be made then. The contributions were for the relief of the Jerusalem church suffering under the ravages of famine possibly in fulfillment of the prophecy of Agabus in Acts 11:28–30. 1 Corinthians 16:1–4 is Paul's account of his responsibility in the collection project (see Acts 11:30). Paul, as apostle to the Gentiles, was to encourage Gentile brothers to support their Jewish brethren in Jerusalem suffering under difficult circumstances. This was a brilliant opportunity to build unity in the faith as well as further ministry within the church.

Interpretations of 1 Corinthians 16:1–3

The first day of the week was the day Paul instructed the Galatian and Corinthian churches to lay aside a sum of money for the project (1 Cor 16:1). No reason is explicitly given for setting aside the money on the first day.[1] Many scholars see here an "implicit indication" in this text of a Christian gathering on the first day on a regular basis.[2] Others see no indication of regular status being given to the first day as a regular day of worship. Bacchiocchi comments, "These attempts to extrapolate from Paul's fund-raising plan a regular pattern of Sunday observance reveal inventiveness and originality, but they seem to rest more on construed arguments than on the actual information the text provides."[3] Marcus Dods also affirms the fruitlessness of pursuing any first day significance from this text by saying, "This verse has sometimes been quoted as evidence that the Christians met for worship on Sundays as we do. Manifestly it shows nothing of the kind."[4]

There is also no consensus why the money was to be set aside on the first day. Bacchiocchi speculates that Paul recommended the first day "for the special fund-raising contributions before other priorities might diminish their resources."[5]. Dods

---

1. Conzelmann, *Acts*, 296; Specht, "Sunday in the New Testament," 125; Rordorf, *Sunday*, 195.

2. Bacchiocchi, *Sabbath to Sunday*, 90, fn.3.

3. Ibid., 93.

4. Dods, *Corinthians*, 712.

5. Bacchiocchi, *Sabbath to Sunday*, 101.

guesses that it occurred "possibly only for some trade reasons now unknown."[6] Willy Rordorf argues the possibility that Paul was "making a special arrangement" in that for this specific occasion it was better to save individually rather than collect corporately at the weekly worship meeting.[7] What does seem clear is that Paul felt that the first day was a good day to make a contribution and set aside money. Why did he see this day as a good time for setting aside money for the contribution?

Why the First Day?

Paul mentions the collection project briefly. His instructions were clearly communicated. The instructions called for each believer to set aside a sum of money once a week, presumably every week. The weekly giving was narrowed to a specific day. At this point is where the significance lies. Paul could have instructed the Corinthians and Galatians to set aside the money once a week regardless of the day. However, he instructed them to do so on one specific day. Why was this the case? Paul probably chose the first day of the week because it would be a day of common significance to all believers in Galatia and Corinth. Paul chose the day where regular weekly offerings were given in public. He requested that during this time they set aside a certain amount in accordance with God's prospering that week. Paul gives no explicit reason why they were to set aside the money on the first day of the week. The time for such an effort was likely understood by those addressed. Therefore, the reason he does not explicitly justify the setting aside of money on the first day is because no explanation was necessary. Paul ordered the setting aside of money to take place on Sunday of all days to guarantee its regularity, because the Christians had already begun to fix their calendar by reference to the weekly Sunday.[8]

Another consideration is the religious nature of the activity. This was an effort to demonstrate stewardship within the

6. Dods, *Corinthians*, 712.
7. Rordorf, *Sunday*, 194.
8. Ibid., 195.

church. Because of the religious nature of the Jerusalem project, a collection from believers for fellow believers, the money would be set aside on the day which held religious significance within the church. The money was set aside on a weekly basis because it corresponded with the weekly time of public offering. This is supported by Paul's insistence the offering be held aside until he arrived. He did not want a collection taken during his visit because he was in a hurry.

The book of Acts records how he would forego his planned stay in Ephesus in order to get to Jerusalem by Pentecost (Acts 20:16). This was a change of plans, for his original plan was to stay in Ephesus for further ministry (1 Cor 16:8–9). Paul wanted to guarantee a sizable gift would be collected from the Corinthians. He wanted to give them time to get representatives ready to accompany him on his trip to Jerusalem (1 Cor 16:3). This was an immense undertaking requiring a high degree of organization. Paul wanted to expedite the project as smoothly and quickly as possible. The inability to satisfactorily explain why Paul chose the first day of the week ignores the obvious reason: the first day of the week was perfect for expediting the gathering of money because it was the day of normal church offerings. Paul's silence on the matter speaks eloquently to this interpretation. Therefore, the evidence both explicit and implicit within the text testifies to it being an indication of regular significance given to the first day of the week.

The Relationship of Acts 20:7–12 and 1 Corinthians 16:1–3

The instructions in 1 Corinthians 16:1–3 are given during the same time frame as another reference to the first day of the week (Acts 20:7–12). A unifying factor bridging both texts may appear when the context of both passages is examined. Both passages deal with the same time period, Paul's third missionary journey (Acts 18:23—21:17). Each reference to the first day is mentioned in association with this period of time. The first day of the week is prominent in that three churches are pictured in some type of involvement on the first day of the week (Troas, Galatia, and Corinth).

The unifying element uniting both passages is Paul's third missionary journey. This is seen by the narrative of Acts in comparison with Paul's first letter to Corinth. In his first letter to Corinth, Paul stated his wish to stay in Ephesus until Pentecost (16:8). However, because of opposition in Ephesus (Acts 19:23–34) which he seemed to anticipate (1 Cor 16:9), Paul had to change his mind about staying in Ephesus until Pentecost. Luke records Paul's change of mind as due to his desire to get to Jerusalem in a hurry (Acts 20:16). Paul states the reason as being "compelled by the Spirit" to get to Jerusalem (Acts 20:22). In 1 Corinthians 16:6, Paul states his intention to stay in Corinth through the winter. This probably corresponds with his stay in Greece for three months mentioned in Acts 20:3. Paul's third missionary journey does not indicate the origin of first day significance. It does indicate that by this time the first day of the week was a day of significance within the Christian church. Acts 20 describes the first day of the week as a day for gathering to worship, fellowship, and hearing the word of God. The meeting in Troas includes the standard biblical descriptions of such a meeting for these purposes.

Since 1 Corinthians 16:2 is set during the same period of time as Acts 20:7, Paul's reference to the first day of the week in 1 Corinthians bears direct relationship with his visit to Troas. Luke describes the meeting at Troas as a Christian worship service where Paul spoke. Paul follows this by using the first day of the week as a chronological reference point for the setting aside of money for the Jerusalem project. The linkage between the two may be due to early church practice of gathering on the first day of the week for Christian worship. Paul stayed long enough in Troas to speak to believers at their regularly appointed meeting. Paul's instruction to the Corinthians strongly connects the offering to the day for public offerings in the church. Therefore, the first day of the week is indicated to be a day for Christian worship, fellowship, and stewardship.

8

THE LORD'S DAY IN REVELATION 1:10

A THEOLOGY of the Lord's Day is not developed in the New Testament but later, beginning especially in the second century. Observance of the Lord's Day was based upon Christ's resurrection on the first day, his resurrection typologically on the "eighth day" (such as the eighth day for circumcision symbolizing a new creation), and the creation of light on the first day of the week during the Genesis creation (*Epistle of Barnabas* 15; Justin, *First Apology* 67). The development of the Lord's Day during its inception was never as a replacement of or substitute for the Jewish Sabbath. More accurately, the Lord's Day was seen as a commemorative time for worship and fellowship rather than a day of rest. The earliest records all indicate that the Lord's Day was also a work day (Acts 20:7; Pliny, *Letter to Trajan*; Justin, *First Apology* 67; Tertullian, *De Oratio* 23). Furthermore, the rationale for the Lord's Day as a day of worship is consistently based upon the resurrection of Jesus on the first day of the week.

A developing theology for the Lord's Day in Christian terms is seen ultimately in the day being referred to as the "Lord's Day." This title is recorded as being incontrovertibly used around the middle of the second century.[1] However, controversy does exist regarding its usage in early second century texts (*Didache* 14:1; Ignatius, *Epistle to the Magnesians* 9:1). In particular, Ignatius' reference to the Lord's Day could go either way depending on what

---

1. Strand, "Another Look," 347; Bauckham, "Lord's Day," 230.

one implies into the text.² Should Ignatius be seen as referring to the Lord's Day, a continuum is established between the earliest usage of the term in Revelation 1:10 and later incontrovertible usage in the mid-second century.

The earliest usage of the "Lord's Day" is Revelation 1:10. There is some debate as to what it refers to within the canon of scripture. The importance of the term cannot be overemphasized. Should it definitely refer to the first day of the week, then at least apostolic recognition of the first day as such is established. That includes the recognition of it as a special day, hence "Lord's Day." It is noteworthy that the language involved in Revelation 1:10 is itself unique. The Greek for "Lord's Day" is *kuriakē hēmera*. The word *kuriakē* is used in one other text in the New Testament respecting the "Lord's Supper" (1 Cor 11:20). This indicates the terminology may be new and fresh, never used to describe such a thing before. This is evidenced by the Lord's Supper, which the Lord himself instituted as a new commemoration of his work on the cross. The point is that such a fresh term used to describe a specific day of the week is truly significant.

There has been scholarly debate over Revelation 1:10 and its meaning. Following will be a discussion and critique of various interpretations of the text. The conclusion will be that the traditional interpretation for the "Lord's Day" referring to the first day of the week merits continued approval. Whether the term refers to a *weekly* observance of the Lord's Day is beside the point. Suffice it to say that recognition of the first day of the week as the Lord's Day necessitates significance given to the day above other days of the week. The overwhelming consensus among Christians who observe the Jewish Sabbath is the reference to "Lord's Day" in Revelation 1:10 refers to anything *but* the first day of the week. This predominate view is supported by various seventh-day scholars using several different alternate interpretations of the phrase *kuriakē hēmera*. These interpretations can be summed as follows.

---

2. Bauckham, "Lord's Day," 229.

1. The "Lord's Day" refers to the eschatological, final "day of the Lord." This position is advocated by several first-day commentators as well as Samuele Bacchiocchi.[3]
2. The Lord's Day refers to an annual Easter Sunday celebration which later developed into a weekly Sunday observance in honor of Christ's resurrection. This view was first advocated by C. W. Dugmore,[4] and has been supported by Seventh Day Adventist scholar Kenneth Strand.[5]
3. The "Lord's Day" refers to the weekly seventh-day Sabbath.
4. Subsidiary considerations mentioned from time to time by commentators on this text are: (1) a possible linkage between "Lord's Day" and a pagan Roman "Emperor's day"; and (2) an association between the "Lord's Day" and the Mithraic worship of the sun.

The above interpretations each have their strengths and weaknesses. Following will be a discussion of their individual weaknesses.

1. The Day of the Lord

Following the traditional interpretation of Revelation 1:10 referring to the weekly Lord's Day, the most popular view among scholars is to view the reference as another way of saying "day of the Lord." Revelation 1:10 simply states that in vision John beheld the second advent of Christ on the Day it occurs. Therefore, John did not see the vision on a particular day of the week but saw in vision the day of the Lord's coming. Bacchiocchi has catalogued the arguments for this view very succinctly. In support of this position, Bacchiocchi lists several reasons in support of "Lord's Day" as the "day of the Lord."

First, the context of the entire book of Revelation is symbolic prophetic imagery. This would include the immediate context of

---

3. Bacchiocchi, *Sabbath to Sunday*, 123-131.
4. Dugmore, "Lord's Day and Easter," 277, 279.
5. Strand, "Another Look," 178-79.

Revelation 1:10. The context is eschatological (1:7-8, 12-18). A threefold time dimension is shown in 1:19 which views history as past, present, and future from a prophetic perspective. The conclusion, therefore, is the reference to "Lord's Day" must necessarily be a symbolic reference rather than literal due to the symbolic context of Revelation itself.[6] Second, the content of John's vision could not have been viewed in a single day. This point assumes the content to be the entire Book of Revelation. Therefore, John could not receive all of this in one sitting, one vision, or one day. Evidence for this is found in 4:2 where John is again seen in vision using terminology similar to 1:10. This indicates John was in vision on another occasion.[7] Third, the language used in Revelation1:10 can be an indication of emphasis. In short, the grammar in "Lord's Day" can put emphasis on "day" rather than "Lord's" in identifying whether attention is given more to the day of the vision or the vision of the day. Thus, to say that John was in the spirit on the Lord's Day would mean that he was actually witnessing the very *day* of the Lord, rather than seeing the vision on a certain day of the week.[8]

Fourth, a comparison of texts (Rev 1:10 with Acts 22:17) reveals a similarity of structure which itself reveals the primary focus of John's vision. First, the verb usage in both passages seems to indicate what was viewed rather than when it was viewed. Paul's vision in Acts 22:17 indicates that Paul saw the Lord. John's vision, on a similar line, indicates he saw the Lord's Day.[9]

Does the interpretation of "Lord's Day" as "day of the Lord" hold up under scrutiny? Many scholars from both the seventh-day and first-day persuasions hold that it does not. Following are a brief list of these problematic areas. Why does not John use the widely-used Greek expression for the "day of the Lord", which is used in the Septuagint and by other New Testament writers? The terminology is similar, but as pointed out by Rordorf, "the difference is in

---

6. Bacchiocchi, *Sabbath to Sunday*, 123-125.
7. Ibid., 125-126.
8. Ibid., 128-129.
9. Ibid., 129.

this instance more important than their similarity."[10] There is more here than a "minor variation"[11] in terminology. The uniqueness of the phrase *kuriakē hēmera* lends to a more concise and specialized usage rather than another way of saying "day of the Lord."

The context of Revelation 1:10 describes a literal setting for the vision. Upon reading Revelation 1 in its entirety, one finds it very difficult to divide the literal situation of the vision from the vision itself. First, the context reveals that John definitely describes the place *where* the vision came (Patmos); *why* he was there (persecution); *who* was exiled (John); *what* John saw (the resurrected Christ in glory); and *when* he received the vision (Lord's Day). Why would John go to such effort to literally *set the stage* for the content of the vision itself and then refer to "Lord's Day" as a symbolic reference? To insist that because the Book of Revelation deals primarily with symbolic imagery automatically means the phrase "Lord's Day" has no literal application is to perhaps make John too esoteric. A proper hermeneutic would dictate a literal understanding where it is meant and a symbolic interpretation where it applies. Revelation 1:10 is not clearly a symbolic text.

The contention is made that John could not have received the entire contents of Revelation in a 24-hour period. Therefore, to understand 1:10 as referring to a literal day is asking too much. A problem arises with such an assertion. First, to assert that John could not have received the contents of Revelation due to time constraints is to assume something which cannot be proven. Who of us has been the recipient of such a visionary experience to test the time factor of such an experience? This assertion is conditioned by the modern scientific mind which seeks to quantify and qualify every phenomenon of existence. Second, the writers of the New Testament clearly recorded their experiences and inspiration at a later date after the experiences and visions were witnessed. Therefore, it is certainly probable that John could receive the visions in one day yet record the content of the visions at a later date.

10. Rordorf, 208.
11. Ibid., 126.

The comparison between Revelation 1:10 and Acts 22:17 is well taken, yet over-emphasized. It ignores one important factor. Paul's experience is clearly described as "I . . . *saw* the Lord speak." John's experience is described as "I was in the Spirit on the Lord's Day, and I *heard* behind me a loud voice." John clearly did not see anything until he turned around in v. 12, yet Bacchiocchi infers that "the immediate result of the vision was for Paul a view of the Lord, while for John that of the Lord's Day."[12] Thus, he believes that John *saw* the Lord's Day just as Paul saw the Lord speak. There is an important difference. John did not see the Lord's Day. He did hear the voice in v. 12, but what he saw was the Lord whom the voice came from, not the day on which it came.

The grammatical usage in 1:10 regarding emphasis upon the day of the vision opposed to the vision of the day is a valid point. However cogent such an argument may be, interpreting its significance remains open. "John's use of the adjective rather than of the noun *may* well reflect his desire to emphasize the very day of Christ's glorious coming into which he was taken in Spirit."[13] Additionally, John does not use the expected Greek terminology for "day of the Lord." This fact seems to neutralize any supposed grammatical trickery inherent in Revelation 1:10.

The "day of the Lord" interpretation, though meriting serious consideration, is not a fully satisfactory interpretation. It has too many problematic areas which are disputable. To state that John was literally in the spirit on a symbolic day seems inconsistent and arbitrary.

2. Annual Easter Sunday

The next and most recent interpretation is that Revelation 1:10 refers to the annual Easter or Passover celebration of the Lord's resurrection. Support for this view is the following considerations. First, there is no firm support for believing the *weekly* first day

12. Ibid., 129.
13. Ibid., 129; emphasis added.

was seen as important by the New Testament writers.[14] Second, certain Lord's Day allusions in the *Didache* and *Apostolic Constitutions* (second century catechism) may refer to an annual rather than weekly first day celebration. Third, baptized Christians took their first communion at Easter which shows that Easter Sunday was preeminent over the weekly Sunday. Fourth, a connection can be made between an annual first day celebration with Jewish Passover traditions. Early Christians adopted the Passover celebration in honor of the risen Christ. First Corinthians 5:7–8 may indicate such an early custom, "For Christ, our paschal lamb, has been sacrificed. Let us, therefore, celebrate the festival."

The above assertions are problematical because of several considerations. First, the annual Passover celebration was in dispute in the Roman province of Asia, the location of John's Revelation. The dispute was over the exact date upon which the Passover should be celebrated, whether Nisan 14 (irrespective of the day on which it fell) or always on the Sunday following Passover. The Asian church believed the celebration should fall on Nisan 14 which rules out a first day observance of the Paschal feast.[15] As Strand has pointed out, even if it is shown that the annual Sunday Passover celebration developed into a weekly celebration, it still "does not solve the problem of Rev i.10."[16] Why? It was due to the Asian church not celebrating the resurrection on the Sunday following the Jewish Passover. Second, it is not clear from the earliest evidence that the annual Easter Sunday celebration preceded the weekly observance of the Lord's Day.[17] If one accepts the New Testament evidence for Lord's Day observance (Acts 20:7; 1 Cor 16:2), it certainly intimates weekly observance preceded or was contemporaneous with annual observance of Easter. Third, evidence is lacking that *kuriakē* refers unambiguously to Easter Sunday.[18] Connected with this is the failure to explain how the annual observance of Easter

---

14. Strand, "Another Look," 174.
15. Bauckham, "Lord's Day," 230-231.
16. Strand, "Another Look," 179.
17. Bauckham, "Lord's Day," 231.
18. Bauckham, "Lord's Day," 230; Aune, *Revelation*, 84.

developed into the weekly Lord's Day observance.[19] To assert that "somehow" the weekly derived from the annual,[20] lacks evidence to support it. Additionally, there is no controversy in the earliest literature debating the merits of observing the annual Easter celebration as opposed to the weekly observance of the Lord's Day.[21] Finally, whether or not observance of the first day of the week was known by the term "Lord's Day" throughout the early church is not at issue. At issue is the assertion that because it wasn't therefore it could not be a regular weekly observance. Such an assertion is not evidenced in the earliest Christian literature which definitely pictures Christians worshipping on the first day of the week, whatever its designation.

Taken together, these factors weigh heavily against interpreting Revelation 1:10 as referring to an annual Easter Lord's Day celebration on the first day of the week.

3. The Seventh Day Sabbath

The general belief among many observers of the Jewish Sabbath is that "Lord's Day" refers to the seventh-day Sabbath. The chief reason for this is due to the fact the Sabbath is referred to as God's holy day (e.g., Isa 58:13 where the Sabbath is called the "Lord's holy day"; and Mark 2:28 where Jesus is Lord of the Sabbath day). These texts are cited as chief proof of this interpretation of Revelation 1:10. There are several problems with such an approach. First, the connection cannot be held on solid hermeneutical grounds. The method of association is the proof-text method which tends to divorce a text from its context. The usage of Mark 2:28 in support of this position is emblematic of this problem. For one, Jesus is not so much labelling the Sabbath as his day (in the possessive sense), but that his authority as Lord extends over that day as an institution of Israel (see v. 27). Thus, his position as Lord allows him to

---

19. Bauckham, "Lord's Day," 231.
20. Strand, "Another Look" 175.
21. Bauckham, "Lord's Day," 231.

have authority over the day itself. Further, there exists no linguistic connection between *kuriakē* (Rev 1:10) and "Lord's holy day" in Isa 58:13, because the Septuagint uses *kuriakē* only in 2 Maccabees 15:36. Second, if John used "Lord's Day" as an alternate expression for the seventh day Sabbath in the Revelation, why did he not use it in his Gospel as an appropriate designation of the Sabbath? It would seem he would since his Gospel was written near the time Revelation was written.

In light of these points, it would seem the Sabbath interpretation of Revelation 1:10 fails. There is no arguing against the idea that the Sabbath was God's holy day. This is not in dispute. What is disputable is whether a commonly understood usage, such as Sabbath, became known by another biblically unique term like "Lord's Day." Nowhere in the New Testament is the Sabbath known as the "Lord's Day." However, the use of "Lord's Day" referring to the first day is incontrovertible by this time and was the prevalent terminology for that day.

4. Further Considerations

The first consideration is an association between "Lord's Day" and a Roman "Emperor's day." In ancient imperial contexts, *kuriakē hēmera* may have referred to a special day or days set aside for veneration of the emperor. If so, John and Asian Christians may have applied this phrase to the day of Christian worship as a deliberate attempt to distinguish between the Lord Caesar and the Lord Jesus Christ because the adjective *kuriakē*, from the root noun *kurios*, meaning Lord or Emperor, was used for all things imperial.[22] Further support is seen in that the Christian population was at odds with the Roman imperial cult by its refusal to worship the imperial image of the Emperor. This was especially the context in which Revelation was written. Thus, the historical situation to which Revelation was written provides reason to believe that "Lord's Day" was a deliberate attempt to contrast imperial power

---

22. Bacchiocchi, *Sabbath to Sunday*, 115.

with the Lordship of Christ.[23] Finally, it is known that an "Emperor's day" did exist in Asian Minor at the time John's Revelation was written.[24]

The second consideration is a possible association between the Mithraic worship of the sun on a particular day and the Christian "Lord's Day." Such a position infers that Christians of John's day (90–100 C.E.) were influenced by pagan sun-worship which was the derivation to the

The Revelation does not demonstrate that Christians syncretize their observances by adopting pagan religious beliefs, such as the worship of the sun. There is no evidence for this in either biblical or immediate post-apostolic literature. Revelation was written to Christians in Asia Minor who were under persecution from the pagan Roman power. It seems unlikely that such an environment would foster adoption of pagan images. Furthermore, persecution often acted as a galvanizing force for fidelity to the gospel in the early church. It was not until times of peace that the church began adopting pagan practices and "Christianizing" them. Rather than arguing for a supposed adoption of Mithraic sun-worship by the early church, it is more likely that John was making a deliberate distinction between a pagan "sun-day" and a Christian "Lord's Day" in order to set Christianity over against pagan practice. With the above propositions analyzed, what alternatives remain? The only alternative left, other than complete mystery, is the traditional interpretation of Revelation 1:10: the "Lord's Day" as a title given to the first day of the week, the regular day of Christian worship.

The Lord's Day as the First Day

What support can be had for the traditional viewpoint? The following considerations are seen as compelling evidence for the traditional interpretation of Revelation 1:10 as referring to the first day of the week. First, the uniqueness of the expression *kuriakē*

23. Ibid., 116.
24. Ibid., 115.

hēmera lends itself to the idea of a new *designation* arising respecting a particular day. This unique Greek phrase suggests a usage and development not previously seen in apostolic Christianity. The event which would inspire such a significant development would be the resurrection of Christ as Lord. Therefore, the development of a "Lord's Day" would not result from simply a commemoration of an event; rather, the event signifies an act of God in salvation history akin to Passover or the Exodus.

Second, the context of Revelation 1:10 strongly suggests that the resurrection event was connected with what John saw in vision and later recorded. Therefore, a linkage can be made between the day on which John saw his vision (the Lord's Day) and what he saw in that vision on that day (the resurrected, glorified Lord). When John turns around in v. 12 in response to the voice speaking to him, he sees the glorified Christ in His resurrected glory as First and Last (v. 17). Verse 18 culminates the vision of Christ by declaring, "I am the *Living One*; I was *dead*, and behold *I am alive for ever and ever*! And I hold the keys of death and Hades." This vision of the resurrected, victorious, and glorified Lord on the Lord's Day can hardly be coincidental.

Third, the rule of historical precedent in arriving at tradition is a powerful fact to consider respecting this matter. Historical precedent simply states that subsequent usage of a term or concept is derived from a common thread of origin. Consistently, in the post-apostolic literature of the mid- to late-second century, the Lord's Day is seen as referring to the first day of the week. "From the later second century onwards it is clear that Sunday was the regular day of Christian worship everywhere, and there is no record of any controversy over whether worship should take place on Sunday."[25]

Admittedly, the material often cited from the early second century as proof the Lord's Day as the first day of the week is controversial and not indisputable, yet *kuriakē hēmera* seemed to be "in fairly widespread use at least in Syria and Asia Minor, designating the first day of the week as the Christian day of regular

---

25. Bauckham, "Lord's Day," 231.

corporate worship."²⁶ However, one must be honest enough to inquire how later usages of Lord's Day became synonymous with the first day of the week. Where did such a precedent occur? The obvious answer is from apostolic recognition. In arguing against the Lord's Day referring to the first day of the week, critics often point out there is no apostolic declaration or precedent for declaring this to be so. This is true, but perhaps this is not the point at all. It can be argued justifiably that the apostles did not always have to authorize a practice in order for the practice to become acceptable tradition.

Tradition in the early church developed over time and received apostolic recognition. Tradition is more fluid than often thought. The apostles wrote letters often addressing problems in the churches without mentioning where or how the problems arose. It is naive to suggest the apostles dictated a formula for every custom in the church. Cultural influences dictate much of what a church does. The apostle's authority would be brought in if a custom or teaching compromised or violated the gospel. If this scenario is correct, then apostolic reference to the Lord's Day carries added weight. What this means is that a custom or tradition, such as Lord's Day observance, may not necessitate or require an apostolic command in order to legitimate its practice. In fact, what John may be doing in Revelation 1:10 is *recognizing* a custom of Lord's Day observance which was *already* practiced in those churches. Obviously, when he wrote that he was in "the spirit" on the Lord's Day, he assumed his readers would understand what he referred to by the phrase. This indicates common understanding of a tradition in place at that time.

It is often pointed out the phrase "Lord's Day" is not seen in John's Gospel or Epistles. If the first day was seen as the Lord's Day, then why did not John refer to the first day as the Lord's Day in his other writings? This is a valid point. However, John's Revelation was addressed specifically to the seven churches in Asia, whereas his Gospel does not seem to be limited to any geographical area. This argument is bolstered by the fact that all the controversial

26. Ibid., 231.

second century references to Lord's Day were addressed to Christians in Asia (*Didache* 14:1; Ignatius, *Epistle to the Magnesians* 9:1).

With the above said in support of a first day interpretation of Revelation 1:10, an observation must be made. The uniqueness of the passage and its language cries not only for attention, but careful consideration. The consideration of the text must be judiciously handled as objectively as possible. It is believed enough has been shown to prompt questioning of each school of interpretation which takes "Lord's Day" as a reference to the seventh day. No approach to interpreting Revelation 1:10 is without problems. The final arbiter for this text is the weight of the evidence. It is believed the weight of evidence stands with the traditional view that the Lord's Day is the first day of the week (Sunday).

9

THE LORD'S DAY
AND THE PAGAN SUNDAY

CONTROVERSY over the origin of the Lord's Day often settles on whether it arose during the time of the apostles or after their deaths. Did it arise in the first century or the second century? What is at stake is biblical legitimacy for the practice of Lord's Day observance *of any kind*. If it arose after the time of the apostles then it stands under indictment as being a post-biblical development. This would render it a Christian observance and tradition lacking biblical support. It would then require explanation as to its origin and legitimacy. If it arose in the first century then it stands under the authority of the apostles and would be biblically based. There would be no need to question its legitimacy.

Much effort has been expended by those who question the biblical basis for Lord's Day observance. They not only doubt its biblical origin, but they cast doubt on the observance of it in any way. They propose a post-biblical origin to the Lord's Day in order to make the observance of it biblically unwarranted. Rather than a biblical origin, they propose a historical genesis independent of apostolic and biblical factors. Typical of such efforts is the frequent appeal to the absence of any apostolic command to observe the first day of the week as a day of Christian worship. Indeed, every rationale given in earliest Christian literature for the observance of the Lord's Day is given in the second century. Because of this no legitimacy is seen in the observance of the Lord's Day in the first century since there are none given.[1] This lack of evidence leads to the conclusion that the Lord's Day is a second century invention.

Another attempt to make Lord's Day observance illegitimate is to contrast it with the Jewish Sabbath. Since the Sabbath is on the seventh day of the week, critics of Lord's Day observance insist that Sunday is an imposter. The contrast is between a Sunday-Sabbath and the true Sabbath. Thus, the Lord's Day is understood as a false, non-biblical day of rest coopting the true seventh day Sabbath. Of course, such an argument infers that the Lord's Day was understood by the early church as a day of rest similar to the Jewish Sabbath. However, such a position is derived more from later Christian history than from early church history.

The historical reconstruction of Lord's Day observance by critics has often taken the shape of pagan influence upon Christian practice, notably the incorporation of the pagan "day of the sun" into Christian tradition. Perhaps the most sophisticated argument for this scenario is one proposed by Samuele Bacchiocchi, a Seventh Day Adventist scholar, in his book *From Sabbath to Sunday*. In this work he proposes a three-fold influence upon the second century church in adopting Sunday as the day of worship. The three influences for the adoption of Sunday were pagan sun worship, anti-Semitism, and Christian desire to separate its identity from Judaism. In assessing the validity of such a proposal it is necessary to examine the central points on which the argument hangs.

Pagan Sun Cults

The notion of pagan sun-worship influencing the origin of Christian Sunday observance overestimates the influence of paganism upon the church of the second century. "Bacchiocchi here underestimates the resistance to pagan customs in second-century Christianity."[2] Strand puts it even more forcefully. "Why would Christians who were ready to give up life itself rather than to adopt

---

1. Bacchiocchi, *Sabbath to Sunday*, 133.
2. Bauckham, "Sabbath and Sunday," 272.

known pagan practices (e.g., Justin Martyr, who did precisely this) choose an obviously pagan Sunday as their Christian day of worship? And how could Christianity so widely—in East as well as West—in a relatively short time have been duped into accepting a purely pagan practice?"[3] Certainly, the influence of paganism upon Christian practices increased after Constantine institutionalized Christianity as the religion of the Roman Empire.[4] However, to infer such influence upon the church in the early second century would have been utterly unthinkable. As Bauckham explains, "It is true that, from Justin onwards, the Fathers exploited the symbolism of the pagan title "Sunday," but to have actually adopted the pagan day as the Christian day of worship *because* it was prominent in the pagan sun cults would have been a very bold step indeed."[5]

Bacchiocchi links the pagan importance of sun worship to Christianity by citing Justin Martyr's mention of Sunday in his *First Apology*. He then concludes, "Why in his brief exposition of the Christian worship did he mention three times 'the day of the Sun'? ... Apparently because the day was venerated by the Romans. By associating Christian worship with both the day and the symbolism of the pagan Sun, Justin, as we suggested earlier, aimed at gaining from the Emperor a favorable appraisal of Christianity."[6] This would place Christian Sunday observance at least around 150 C.E. Thus, Bacchiocchi concludes that the rise of Sunday observance by Christians coincided with the rise of Sun worship among pagans.

Justin was not attempting to gain a favorable impression from the Emperor. Rather, he was merely citing Sunday as the day when Christians gathered to worship. He referred to Sunday as a familiar reference point for pagans, not to win appraisal from them. There is no indication whatever that his reference to Sunday had anything to do with Christian adoption of a pagan day of veneration. Justin identified the Christian day of worship as Sunday so the Emperor

3. Strand, "Another Look," 90.
4. Bauckham, "Sabbath and Sunday," 272; Strand, "Another Look," 90-91.
5. Bauckham, "Sabbath and Sunday," 272.
6. Bacchiocchi, *Sabbath to Sunday*, 251.

would know which day Christians gathered for worship. He was explaining Christian custom, not reflecting Christian adoption of paganism. This explanation betrays Bacchiocchi's greatest weakness for a pagan Sunday influence on the Christian Lord's Day in the second century. By the time of Justin, the observance of the Christian Sunday was already well established. Justin is not drawing a parallel between Christian worship on Sunday and the pagan Sunday as if the Christian Sunday is new. Rather, he draws attention to Christian worship on Sunday because it was already the Christian day of worship.

He mentions Sunday three times. The first reference is "on the day called Sunday." Why did he call it the "day called Sunday"? Did he do so to show similarity to the pagan sun cults or pagan calendar or pagan observance? He referred to it because on Sunday "all who live in cities or in the country gather together to one place" to worship God. Furthermore, it is "the day on which we all hold our common assembly, because it is the first day on which God . . . made the world; and Jesus Christ our Saviour on the same day rose from the dead." Finally, Sunday was the day when Jesus "appeared to His apostles and disciples (teaching) them these things." Justin twice mentions the pagan name for the Jewish Sabbath (Saturn). It too acts as a reference point to Sunday. Justin refers to the "day before that of Saturn" and to the "day after that of Saturn, which is the day of the Sun." Why did Justin not refer to it as the Jewish Sabbath? If Bacchiocchi is correct about pagan influence on the Christian Sunday, then does Justin's reference to Saturn mean he wanted to demonstrate pagan influence on the Sabbath? Why did Justin refer to both the pagan names for the Sabbath and the Lord's Day? The audience dictated his terminology. He was writing to a pagan Roman emperor using calendar names for days familiar to him. It was not to demonstrate any similarities to pagan sun cults or traditions. They act as points of reference, not parallel traditions.

If the foregoing is the case, then Bacchiocchi's argument falls apart. What Justin's account actually demonstrates is the Christian observance of the Lord's Day on the pagan day of the sun. *Simply because the two days carry importance for both sides does not mean the pagan gave birth to the Christian day of worship.* Rather, Justin clearly states the rationale for Christian observance of the Lord's Day, though he calls it Sunday, as based upon *acts of God*—one being the first day of creation and the other being the resurrection. This strongly indicates the rationale for Christian Sunday observance as being based on scripture and the historical timing of the resurrection, not adoption of pagan traditions. Justin's account is a *distinctly Christian account* of events occurring on Sunday.

The Christian struggle against pagan persecution and influence in the first two centuries of the Christian era stands as formidable evidence against Bacchiocchi's theory. Christians did not adopt pagan beliefs and traditions in order to verify Christian beliefs. Christian apologists may have cited parallels between Christian beliefs and pagan traditions, yet they did so to demonstrate the truthfulness and superiority of the Christian tradition. Though paganism influenced some Christians to believe unorthodox things (e.g. Gnosticism), the tenor of Christian apologetics was to differentiate Christianity from paganism. "The desire to differentiate from paganism had deeper Christian roots than the second-century desire for differentiation from Judaism."[7]

Another text referring to Christian worship on Sunday is found in Tertullian's *Ad Nationes* 13 (ca. 145–220 C.E.). The reference deals directly with the charge that Christian worship on Sunday is connected to pagan sun worship.

> Others, with greater regard to good manners, it must be confessed, suppose that the sun is the god of the Christians, because it is a well-known fact that we pray towards the east, or because we make Sunday a day of festivity . . . It is you, at all events, who have even admitted the sun into the calendar of the week; and you have selected its day, in preference to the preceding day as the most suitable in the week . . . [Y]ou who reproach us with the sun and Sunday should consider your proximity to us.

Bacchiocchi asserts that Tertullian avoided using "sun-symbology to justify the Christian Sunday" for two reasons. First, it

---

7. Bauckham, "Sabbath and Sunday," 272.

would have "supported the pagan accusation that Christians were Sun-worshipers (a charge he strongly resented)." Second, Tertullian was "cognizant of the influence which pagan festivals still had on the Christians." "Therefore, any attempt to associate the day of the Sun with the Christian Sunday, at a time when the latter was still a young institution, could have been readily misinterpreted by Christians still susceptible to pagan influences."[8] Whatever the reasons may have been, the point is that he strongly refuted any association between Christian worship on Sunday with pagan veneration of the day. "In these passages Tertullian is controverting the erroneous opinion of pagans that Christians were sun-worshippers because they prayed towards the rising sun and spent Sunday joyously."[9] Furthermore, Christians were "suspected of being sun-worshippers (because) . . . they prayed towards the east and that the day of the sun had an especial significance for them."[10]

Sunday held special significance for Christians, but not in connection to paganism. If Christian worship on Sunday had been pagan influenced, would Tertullian have denounced the charge so insistently? The pagans were under the impression that Christians were sun-worshippers because of their prayer habits. This was merely one of many misunderstandings in pagan knowledge of Christian habits, and one which was not true. Therefore, Tertullian was setting the record straight that no pagan sun-cult influence had conditioned Christian practice. Though early Christian writers used sun imagery to communicate truth about Jesus,[11] it remains to be proven that Christians appropriated the pagan veneration of Sunday as originating the custom of Lord's Day observance. This is precisely the claim Bacchiocchi makes,

> Does not the fact that Christ was early associated in iconography and in literature (if not in actual worship) with the *Sol invictus*—Invincible Sun, suggest the possibility that even the day of the Sun could readily have been

---

8. All quotes from Bacchiocchi, *Sabbath to Sunday*, 263.
9. Rordorf, *Sunday*, 157, fn. 4.
10. Ibid., 158.
11. Bacchiocchi, *Sabbath to Sunday*, 252-256.

adopted for worshiping Christ, the *Sol iustitiae*—the Sun of Justice? It would require only a short step to worship Christ-the-Sun, on the day specifically dedicated to the Sun.[12]

The "possibility that even the day of the Sun could readily have been adopted for worshiping Christ" is only possible if Christians in the early second century had no day of worship, except perhaps the Jewish Sabbath, yet would appropriate a *pagan* day of worship with no scriptural warrant (except that which is contrived), and adopt it as a *Christian* day for worship. Such a scenario pictures the early church as willing to compromise its anti-pagan stance by readily adopting the day of pagan worship minus the pagan god in order to worship Jesus.

Such a move would be momentous for the early church. It alludes to a conspiracy to change the day of Christian worship by selling out to paganism in order to be less Jewish. However, there is no instance where the stated reasons for Christian worship on Sunday in the earliest Christian literature gives adoption of pagan custom as the reason for Sunday worship. If such a transition had occurred, why would no one mention it. Bacchiocchi is left with "possibilities" which require negative assumptions of Christian motivations. Furthermore, it is no "short step" to arriving at adoption of the pagan day of the sun from using sun imagery to picture the work of Christ. Bacchiocchi has set up a straw man in assuming Christians in the early post-apostolic church were desperate to find a day of worship opposite of the Jewish Sabbath and then compromising enough to adopt the pagan day of worship. It must be proven that early Christians of this time did not worship on Sunday from purely *Christian* reasons.

Perhaps the greatest assumption in Bacchiocchi's scenario is viewing the universal church following suit without one complaint. "Even if the church of Rome had taken this step, it becomes even more inexplicable that the rest of the church followed suit without argument."[13] The early church could not come to a universal

12. Ibid., 253-254.
13. Bauckham, "Sabbath and Sunday," 272.

agreement on when Easter should be celebrated, either on Nisan 14 or on the Sunday following it. If the church debated the date for the yearly celebration of Christ's resurrection, then would not the adoption of the weekly pagan day of the sun elicit even stronger controversy in the church?

Primacy of the Roman Church

In order for a supposed adoption of the pagan Sunday to be accomplished the authority of the Roman church must have been substantial. Bacchiocchi's thesis hinges on this assumption. "It was the preeminent authority of the bishop of Rome that influenced the entire church to adopt this new practice" of Lord's Day observance.[14] However, such authority for the Roman bishop was not manifested during the time Bacchiocchi asserts the adoption of Sunday took place (prior to 150 AD). Hence, Bauckham believes this "is probably the weakest of Bacchiocchi's arguments."[15] Only this assertion of the primacy of Rome can begin to explain how a custom originating in the early second century could have become as universal in the Christian church as Sunday worship did.[16] The authority of the Roman church in the second century was important, but not dominant. "That the bishop of Rome later had the jurisdictional authority which Bacchiocchi ascribes to him in the second century is not in dispute."[17] The inability of the Roman bishop later to settle the Easter date controversy betrays the weakness of Bacchiocchi's argument.[18]

Was the Roman Church's success in the second century greater regarding the weekly Sunday, or were other factors operative in its dissemination—factors which Bacchiocchi may have missed? It is important in this connection to observe that during the third

---

14. Ibid., 271.
15. Ibid., "Sabbath and Sunday," 271.
16. Ibid., 271.
17. Strand, "Another Look," 98.
18. See Ibid., 96-98.

through fifth centuries there is evidence of widespread observance of both Sabbath and Sunday rather than the substitution of the Sabbath for Sunday, the practice called to attention by Bacchiocchi for Rome.[19] This fact brings up an intriguing issue. If Christianity had been as intent on separating itself from Judaism by substituting the pagan Sunday for the Jewish Sabbath, then the evidence from the third through fifth centuries testify the effort was a gross failure. Furthermore, "Bacchiocchi leaves the impression that Rome's substitution of Sunday for the Sabbath in the early second century spread quickly, becoming universal in the West, though being somewhat retarded in the East."[20] If such were the case, one would assume evidence of universal Sunday observance would be seen. However, Christians were observing both Sabbath and Sunday throughout the Roman Empire up to the fifth century.[21]

Bacchiocchi's historical construction for the rise of Sunday observance as a counter to Sabbath observance in the early church falls on its face in view of the fact that many continued to observe the Sabbath much later. The authority of the Roman church and bishop to influence Sunday observance based on a pagan borrowing does not stand up. Therefore, the distancing of the church from Judaism which Bacchiocchi supposes through the transference of the pagan Sunday for the Sabbath was not extremely successful. The basic conclusion is that no "church of that period (second century) had sufficient authority to change the weekly day of worship throughout Christendom."[22] The fact that many Christians observed the Jewish Sabbath in the first centuries of the Christian church does not threaten the rise of Lord's Day observance because Lord's Day observance arose on its own terms not linked with the Sabbath. The reason no single church had authority to change the weekly day of worship in the second century is because no change was necessary. Lord's Day observance already existed from the first century. Justifications for Lord's Day observance were consistently

19. Ibid., 99.
20. Ibid., 100.
21. See Ibid., 100, esp. fn. 29.
22. Bauckham, "Sabbath and Sunday," 271.

based on scripture, not adoption of or similarities to pagan practices. It therefore seems extremely unlikely that already in the early second century the authority of the Roman see was such that it could impose Sunday worship throughout the church, superseding a universal practice of Sabbath observance handed down from the apostles, without leaving any trace of controversy or resistance in the historical records.[23]

The reason no trace of evidence remains is because other issues took prominence over the issue of *weekly* Sunday observance, such as Easter and the Sabbath fast.[24] Because of this one can arrive at only two conclusions: either weekly Sunday observance was not an issue because it did not exist, or it was not an issue because it already existed and was observed. If one opts for the first position then explanation for its origin must be given. However, if the second is true then weekly Sunday observance was not a disputed issue because it already arose at an earlier time. This reveals Bacchiocchi's key weakness. The silence about the weekly Sunday assumes its existence prior to Bacchiocchi's timetable.

Anti-Semitism

There is no disputing that the contrasting of Sabbath to Sunday occurred in the second century. However, to state that anti-Sabbatarian bias led to the origin of Sunday is another matter. For one, no evidence exists that early Christians prior to Constantine viewed the Lord's Day as a rest day. This is interesting insofar as Christians early on saw Sunday as a day for worship which existed side by side with Christian seventh day Sabbath observance.[25] This indicates Christian observance of Sunday stood on a different footing than Christian Sabbath observance.

This brings up an interesting dilemma for Bacchiocchi. The title of his book, *From Sabbath to Sunday*, betrays the dilemma.

---

23. Ibid., 272.
24. Bauckham, "Sabbath and Sunday," 272.
25. Strand, "Another Look," 100.

The transition from the Jewish Sabbath to the Christian Sunday entailed more than switching the day of Sabbath observance. Bacchiocchi assumes "that Sunday originated as a Christian Sabbath, a day of worship *and rest*, and therefore an alternative to the Jewish Sabbath."[26] Such an assumption is unwarranted and inaccurate because the Christian Sunday was not a rest day until *after* Constantine. Strand concisely states the difficulty in Bacchiocchi's position.

> The earliest Christian observance of Sunday was for worship (a role which for several centuries, and widely throughout Christendom, it held *side by side* with the Sabbath); only in post-Constantinian times did it become a day of rest (which it did basically in *substitution* for the Sabbath). Even the second-century Roman substitution to which Bacchiocchi calls attention did not involve making Sunday a day of rest.[27]

The above observation creates a situation which makes Bacchiocchi's entire thesis untenable. Why would the early church seek to create another day of rest when many Christians already observed the Jewish Sabbath? The development of Sunday observance (if one can call it that) was only as a time commemorating the event which occurred on that day, the resurrection. The day itself became important for Christian observance only because of the event that occurred on it. Thus, the genesis of the Christian Sunday was far different and simpler than what would become of it centuries later. In the first and second century, Sunday formed alongside the already existent observance of the Sabbath and would only later (in the fourth century) substitute for the Sabbath. Therefore, the church in the second century did not intend for Sunday to take over for the Sabbath, but justified its observance by differentiating it from the Sabbath.

Bacchiocchi creates a situation where Christians wanted to distance themselves from Judaism by creating another day of worship borrowed from paganism cloaked in Christian theology. Such

---

26. Bauckham, "Sabbath and Sunday," 270.
27. Strand, "Another Look," 100.

an approach is unnecessary when it is conceded that Sunday developed alongside the already existent Jewish Sabbath. Christians observed the Lord's Day for completely different reasons than the Sabbath. As time progressed Sabbath observance declined under varying influences, chief of which was the unbiblical change of Sunday into a rest day. It was this change in character which precipitated the rapid decline in Sabbath observance by the sixth century.

It is true that second-century Christian writers viewed the Sabbath negatively.[28] However, to state it motivated Christians to adopt another day to *replace* the Sabbath reads into the evidence what is not there. "Anti-Judaism played its part in second-century Christian polemic against Jewish Sabbath observance, but it does not follow that it motivated the introduction of Christian Sunday worship."[29] Furthermore, in the literature against the Sabbath there is a notable absence of Sunday set up as the alternative to the Sabbath. Why? It was never meant to replace it. "Derogatory discussions of the Jewish Sabbath do not usually refer to the Christian Sunday. If Sunday were a recent substitute for the Jewish Sabbath, we should expect far more discussion of the superiority of Sunday to the Sabbath."[30]

Final Considerations

Bacchiocchi has demonstrated ingenuity in attempting to develop an origin for the Christian Sunday after the first century. It is at this point where his real motivations become clear. Significant effort to deny biblical evidence for Sunday observance was undertaken in his work. The treatment of Acts 20:7, 1 Corinthians 16:1–2, and Revelation 1:10 denied that any first century significance was seen for Sunday in the apostolic church. Because of this, Bacchiocchi, and any person denying first century Sunday observance, must

---

28. Bauckham, "Sabbath and Sunday," 271.
29. Ibid.
30. Ibid.

attempt to derive Sunday observance from another source. Being a believer in the seventh day Sabbath automatically conditions bias against any biblical origin to Sunday observance.

The genesis for Bacchiocchi's work originates from this mindset. However, the effort to deny biblical evidence for Sunday observance is off base. First, the historical evidence demonstrates that the early church saw Christian worship on Sunday as something distinct from Sabbath observance. It was observed for different reasons. It had a different character. It commemorated an event which occurred on Sunday. Second, Sunday itself is not commanded to be observed, unlike the Sabbath, yet the day provides Christians the opportunity to celebrate the decisive act in salvation history, the resurrection of Christ. Third, though Sunday was gradually seen as an alternative to Sabbath observance, this was due more to the increase in the number of Gentiles in the church who were not required to observe the Sabbath. Fourth, the Christian Sunday provided a distinctive day for Christian worship without connection to Jewish law.[31] Fifth, once the early church began to be distinct from Judaism it was only a matter of time before Christian observances would predominate. The derivation of such customs often was influenced by Jewish tradition (Easter/Passover), yet Sunday apparently did not develop as an extension of Sabbath theology and tradition. It became more like the Sabbath only over time. Finally, the differing character of Sunday from the Sabbath would in time be a symbol of the gravitation of Christianity away from Judaism. However, this in no way intimates that Sunday was deliberately invented to create or encourage the gravitation away from Judaism.

The Christian Sunday arose in the first century as a result of one factor, the resurrection of the Lord Jesus Christ. Though other second century theologies developed to explain why Sunday was observed (eighth day, first day of creation), the primary reason throughout is the resurrection on the first day of the week. No other event can account for the first Jewish Christians adopting another day for worship. Furthermore, the fact that the Sabbath

---

31. Ibid., 270.

was not the primary day of worship in the early church betrays the early origin of the Christian Sunday. For example, Justin's account of Christian worship practices on Sunday should not be seen as only detailing Christian practice in Rome. Rather, the account was probably meant to describe Christian practices common to worship services everywhere on Sunday, as his words suggest: "But Sunday is the day on which *we all* hold our common assembly."[32] This is supported in Justin's introduction where he states "this address and petition [is presented] in behalf of those of all nations who are unjustly hated and wantonly abused."[33]

In the face of this counterevidence, Bacchiocchi's scenario falls apart at certain key points. His entire argument is based on several legs. If any one leg is weak or broken, then the entire edifice crashes down. Therefore, the conclusion of this study is that Bacchiocchi has developed "historical reconstructions of the patristic period that read out from isolated and ambiguous expressions massive theological schemes that in reality developed only much later."[34] The crisscrossing of evidence only succeeds in making a second century Sunday origin not only unlikely, but untenable.

---

32. Justin Martyr, *First Apology*, 67 (*The Ante-Nicene Fathers* 1:186).
33. Ibid., 1 (*The Ante-Nicene Fathers* 1:163).
34. Carson, "Introduction," 16.

Appendix 1

THE "FIXED DAY" IN PLINY'S LETTER TO TRAJAN

PLINY's letter to Trajan[1] contains the earliest non-Christian account of Christian worship practices. Included is one of the earliest post-apostolic references to Christians gathering on a particular day for worship. The reference to Christians gathering on a "fixed day" has historically been interpreted as referring to Sunday.[2] However, others have suggested the "fixed day" could refer to Easter or the Jewish Sabbath.[3]

In view of the potential importance of Pliny's letter to understanding the Lord's Day and the difficulties in both the Easter and Sabbath interpretations of the "fixed day", it seems wise to take another look at the reference itself. Examination of the background of the letter will be followed by discussion of the Easter and Sabbath interpretations. The final section will examine the traditional Sunday interpretation of the text and its importance to the ongoing Sabbath-Sunday debate.

---

1. Pliny, *Letters and Panegyricus* II, Books VIII–X.

2. McArthur. *Christian Year*, 18; Willy Rordorf. *Sunday*, 202, 204; Jewett, *Lord's Day*, 69.

3. For the Easter view see Lawrence Geraty, "The Pascha," 87–90; The Sabbath proposal is by Samuele Bacchiocchi, *Sabbath to Sunday*, 99.

APPENDIX 1

Background

Bithynia was a Roman province located on the south coast of the Black Sea in northern Asia Minor. Peter addresses his first letter to believers in Bithynia (1 Peter 1:1). First Peter is dated no later than 67–68 C.E., but probably written between 60–68 C.E. By the time of Pliny's letter (112 C.E.), the Bithynian church had existed for about fifty years. Pliny comments that Christianity was a superstition that penetrated both the urban and rural areas of the province. Christian teaching had indeed pervaded to every sector of society.

It is noteworthy that the charges brought upon the Christians as a *hetaeria* (secret group or club), originated from the non-Christian population. Apparently, the Christians had enough prominence to warrant suspicion. This was not simply a new occurrence. The pagans in Bithynia, as well as other provinces, had accused Christians of wrongdoing (cf. 1 Peter 2:12). By C.E. 112, this was an unusual occurrence for most of the Roman Empire. "In most areas of the Roman Empire Christians lived quietly and peaceably among their neighbors conducting their affairs without disturbance."[4] It seems that legal action was brought against Christians only where friction existed between pagans and believers.

Pliny does not describe the specific charges brought against the Christians, but we can attempt to ascertain their character. There was a universal imperial declaration against the gathering of groups or associations (*hetaeria*) in the Empire. The Christians, who were known to gather together, were suspected of unlawful and perhaps clandestine secret rights.[5] Based upon these accusations, Pliny had to judge the reliability of these charges by interrogating suspected Christians.

Once brought in to be interrogated by Pliny, the accused Christians were tested regarding their sincerity as Christians. Pliny ordered an image to the emperor be brought in along with images to the gods. Pliny understood that true Christians would

---

4. Wilken, *The Christians*, 16.
5. Ibid, 15–25.

not worship these images, so he ordered them to worship them. Those who did not pray, offer incense, and curse the name of Christ proved to be the real Christians. Many were executed after confessing to being Christian after three chances under threat.

What is interesting about the confession of the accused Christians is that they were made by *former* Christians who had departed the faith over a period extending to twenty years.[6] Those who had abandoned Christianity twenty years before probably had done so under the persecution of Domitian, 81–96 C.E.[7]

Their confession consisted of the following characteristics. They had in the past met together as a group prior to daylight on a "fixed day." At the assembly they sang hymns of worship to Jesus as they would to a god.[8] They committed themselves to an oath not to steal, commit adultery, lie, nor neglect to give to one another. After this they would depart and meet again later the same day to eat. Of note in the description is the detail given about the time of day the meeting took place and what occurred at the meetings. However, particularly absent is any reference to which day the observance took place. The day was "fixed" so that the Christians knew when to meet, yet even the former Christians interrogated did not reveal the day it occurred. Apparently no more was revealed by the torturing of the women. Pliny's conclusion was that Christianity was nothing more than a perverted superstition.

The Easter Interpretation

One suggestion for the identity of the "fixed day" is the annual Easter Sunday celebration.[9] The argument suggests the Romans would not have been threatened by the Christian custom of meeting on a weekly basis, no more than they were threatened by the

6. Odom, "Sabbath and Sunday," 73.

7. Ibid., 74.

8. "Like a good Roman, Pliny is simply saying that the Christians have a god of their own; his name is Christ, and they worship him" (van Beeck, "Worship of Christians," 124).

9. Geraty, "The Pascha," 88–90.

APPENDIX 1

Jewish weekly observance of the Sabbath, but would have been threatened by an annual celebration giving "divine honors to some person other than the Roman emperor."[10]

This scenario seems unlikely. Though the frequency of the gatherings is not given, it doubtless occurred more than once a year. The description of the meeting in Pliny's letter is too reminiscent of the description of the Christian worship service in Justin's letter to merely dismiss as describing a yearly celebration. The events at the meeting seem descriptive of a regular gathering (singing, an oath of fidelity, gathering again to eat).[11] The nature of the complaints against the Christians from Bithynian citizens suggests frequent meetings. Pliny does not elucidate the nature of the charges,[12] yet some of them certainly concerned what occurred in the meetings. This suggests the meetings were frequent enough to merit notice from the local citizenry. The rapid growth of Christianity in the local area suggests widespread suspicion of Christian practices.

Geraty argues that Roman reaction to the time of the meeting seemingly indicates an annual Easter observance. On the contrary, evidence within the letter indicates Pliny was concerned about the meeting itself and what occurred in it, rather than the time of the meeting. The mystery regards when the meeting occurred, not Pliny's concern about when it occurred. Geraty regards the contents of the meeting as a "lesser" concern on the part of the Romans. However, evidence indicates it was an important concern. Finally, the major concern focuses on the confession of the meeting, not the time of the meeting. The attention was on *who* the meeting focused on (adoration of Christ as divine), not upon *when* it occurred. Would not the Christians express their worship

---

10. Ibid, 88–89.

11. van Beeck notes, "The vague reference, in the singular, to the 'fixed day', while conveying Pliny's unfamiliarity with the Christians' calendar, suggests regularity, such as that of the first day of the week" ("Worship of Christians," 125).

12. Wilken, *The Christians*, 15.

of Christ as a god on a weekly basis? It is extremely unlikely they waited for a year to express such adoration.

The Sabbath Interpretation

Samuele Bacchiocchi holds to the possibility that the "fixed day" may be the Jewish Sabbath. "In the light of this excursus we conclude that the 'appointed day' of Pliny is not necessarily the selfsame day of the week, unless it was the Sabbath, which possibly Pliny prefers not to mention to avoid placing Christians in a worse light by associating them with Jews . . . [which] would have encouraged the emperor to take harsher measures, the very thing Pliny's letter wished to discourage."[13]

Such a possibility is unlikely for the Bithynian Christians were probably not Jewish in character. This points to the Christians in Bithynia as having their own distinct identity from that of Judaism. "There is no hint that the Christians had anything to do with Jews or that they came from Jewish background. It is likely that some were converted Jews, but Pliny treated the Christians as an independent sect."[14] Because of the largely Gentile makeup of the Bithynian church,[15] it is difficult to definitely see any Sabbath reference in the "fixed day." One may insist these Gentile Christians kept the Sabbath which seems highly unlikely in view of the fact that upon Pliny's edict forbidding the existence of clubs (*hetaeria*), the observance of the day of worship was abandoned

---

13. Bacchiocchi, *Sabbath to Sunday*, 99.
14. Wilken, *The Christians*, 23.
15. "Asia Minor . . . was (a) focal point of missionary activity in the Empire during the second century A.D . . . This rapid and intensive spread of Christianity was responsible for the early outbreak of conflicts with non-Christians (cf. Acts 19:23–40). This was especially so because the Jews in the region distanced themselves pointedly from the Christians . . . I Peter clearly presupposes a predominantly Gentile Christian circle of readers." Jews distanced themselves from the new Christian sect which caused Jewish and Gentile Christians to unite in communities where Gentiles quickly became dominant (Goppelt, *1 Peter*, 6).

by the Christians. If it had been the Sabbath there certainly would have been more than a simple abandonment of these gatherings.

It seems more likely that the abandonment of this day in obedience to Pliny's edict was not a moral issue for the Christians, but one of personal choice. The day itself did not have inherently moral import. If it had, we could expect to see the Christians "drawing the line" where Sabbath was concerned. It would have been similar to Acts 5:29: "Peter and the other apostles replied: 'We must obey God rather than men!'" Clearly, the persecution of these Bithynian Christians was because they were Christians, not because of which day they observed. Bacchiocchi seems to imply that Pliny prefers not to mention Sabbath as the "fixed day" so as to save the Christians from further unjust persecution as Jewish followers. It would seem truer to the context that Pliny would have surely mentioned if it were Sabbath because of its association with Judaism.[16]

The Sunday Interpretation

Bacchiocchi contends that it could not have been the first day of the week for several reasons. The Latin *stato die* (fixed day) can mean a day fixed from week to week, but not necessarily the *same* day from week to week. "The gathering then could occur periodically but not necessarily on the self-same day."[17] The context suggests two possible understandings. The Christians were being accused before Pliny arrived. To avoid suspicion, the Christians may have "changed the day and place of their gathering."[18] After torture and interrogation the governor only found out the time of the day and manner of worship, yet not the day itself. Thus, "Christians in Bithynia were already gathering regularly on Sunday, they would have confessed this as they disclosed the rest of their worship activities."[19] Why?

16. Jewett, *Lord's Day*, 70.
17. Bacchiocchi, *Sabbath to Sunday*, 98.
18. Ibid., 98.
19. Ibid., 99.

In 150 C.E. Justin Martyr used "the day of the Sun" as a rationale for gathering to worship, "apparently as a means of creating a favorable impression."[20] Thus, if the Christians were worshipping on Sunday in Pliny's time, they would have mentioned it to Pliny to gain a favorable impression. If Pliny had found that they gathered on the day of the Sun, would he not presumably have mentioned this fact in order to present the Christian worship in a more favorable light?[21]

Bacchiocchi's point regarding the *stato die* is valid in that it is not specific. Yet, he has chosen to take one alternative (not the same day), and neglected the other (a fixed day week to week). He has merely chosen one of two alternatives. However, the implications of his argument are profound. First, if these Christians did meet together regularly, but on alternate days, then what becomes of the practice of Sabbath and Sunday observance? If they are alternating days then it is quite difficult to see how the Christians could observe a weekly "fixed day" of worship, whether Sabbath or Sunday. Second, such a position indeed opens up the argument that early Christians in Bithynia did not observe any particular day as of special significance above another. They were simply alternating days of gathering to "avoid cause of suspicion."[22] With the above considerations, it is indeed "possible that Christians every week changed the day and place of their gathering,"[23] yet not probable. It would seem the day remained the same because of its "fixed" character.

Bacchiocchi argues that had the Christians been gathering on Sunday, Pliny would have made note of it because worship on Sunday was looked upon as venerated with prestige. Thus, he would have noted it to "present the Christian worship in a more favorable light."[24] Pliny would have found out about it because "they would have confessed this as they disclosed the rest of their worship

---

20. Ibid., 99.
21. Ibid., 99.
22. Ibid., 99.
23. Ibid., 99.
24. Ibid., 99.

APPENDIX 1

activities" in order to gain favorable treatment.[25] Bacchiocchi then cites the appeal made by Justin Martyr (150 C.E.) to the emperor that "the Christians gathered on 'the day of the Sun,' apparently as a means of creating a favorable impression."[26]

Is it conceivable that Bithynian Christians, had they worshipped on Sunday, would use the same rationale to justify worship to Pliny as Justin did to impress the emperor several decades later? While it remains questionable that Justin would mention Sunday to gain a favorable impression, such a claim for Pliny's letter is presupposed and reasons that the same psychology existed with the Bithynian Christians as with the Christians of Justin's time. The citation of Justin's rationale should not be transferred to the situation in Bithynia 30 years earlier. The situation of Christians in Bithynia in 112 C.E. was different than that of Rome in 150 C.E. Bacchiocchi notes that a connection between Paul's writings to Bithynian Christian Sunday worship is thin due to 50 years separating Paul's and Pliny's letter, and "that during that period of time, as we shall notice, changes could readily have occurred."[27] The same point could be argued respecting Pliny's and Justin's letters.

The situation is different between Pliny's and Justin's time in that the Bithynian Christians nowhere sought to accommodate Pliny's interrogations by conceding or justifying their practice by citing pagan similarities. Indeed, the opposite occurred. It should be further noted that the information Pliny received about the manner of Christian worship originated from former believers, not contemporary Christians. This is further seen by the fact that those Christians who confessed three times to being Christian were led away to execution. The former believers cursed the name of Christ, and worshipped Trajan's statue and the images of the gods. There is simply no hint in Pliny's letter that the genuine Christians compromised or justified their practice by appealing to pagan similarities.

25. Ibid., 99.
26. Ibid., 99.
27. Ibid., 98.

Fifty years prior to this the Bithynian believers had confronted a similar situation about which they received instruction from Peter regarding how they were to act toward civil authorities (see 1 Peter 1:17; 2:12; 3:14–15; 4:14–16). "It has long been recognized that the famous letter of the Younger Pliny to Trajan concerning the trials of Christians has important bearing on the understanding of 1 Peter."[28] The similarity of the two situations demonstrates that Bithynian believers continued to show fidelity to Peter's counsel. Bacchiocchi's belief pictures the Christians as eventually compromising their faith by seeking better relations with the State. There is certainly a conflict here. The genuine Christians present a picture of non-compromise, even to death. Pliny was not doing the Christians any favor which leads to the final point.

Why did Pliny make his "cautious" appeal? Was it merely because the condemnation "was causing their killing without regard to their age, sex or attitude?"[29] Certainly it was one of the reasons. However, Trajan's reply to Pliny's letter indicates the real issue was one of *legality* and *public relations*. Legally, Pliny was correct to only punish those who were convicted of being Christian through the test he set up of triple confession under threat. In public relations, Trajan saw an inconsistency in Roman justice when *anyone* who was seen as a Christian was punished. Many non-Christians were unjustly condemned. Hence, anonymous lists of names were further forbidden. They set a bad example unworthy of Roman toleration and justice. We see here Roman bureaucracy at its best.

The point is to show that Bacchiocchi's contention that Pliny would have included any reference to Sunday to facilitate better treatment of Christians is not cogent. Additionally, Pliny did not appeal for the Christians. He appealed for a better method of facilitating justice. He was a bureaucrat, and a good one at that. He sought to create a better method of handling the charges against the Christians by appealing to Trajan's desire for better handling

---

28. See John Knox's excellent discussion of the relationship, "Pliny and 1 Peter: A Note on 1 Peter 4:14–16 and 3:15." *Journal of Biblical Literature* 72 (1953) 187–189.

29. Bacchiocchi, *Sabbath to Sunday*, 99.

of the anti-Christian law. The enforcement of the law had created inequities which resulted in many wrong decisions.

Trajan praised Pliny for his handling of the Christian situation. "You have followed the right course of procedure, my dear Pliny, in your examination of the cases of persons charged with being Christians."[30] Therefore, the central issue was not better treatment for Christians, or presenting "the Christian worship in a more favorable light,"[31] but one of better facilitation of the existing anti-Christian law. In a sense, they wanted to "streamline" the law and make it more effective.

Bacchiocchi's main weakness in this area is his belief that "the anti-Christian law . . . was causing their [that is, Christian] killing without regard to their age, sex or attitude."[32] The issue was not one of leniency to Christians themselves, but of mistakes made to non-Christians because of an inept procedure of determining who was a Christian. Pliny was praised by Trajan for his innovation in handling the charges, not in showing leniency to Christians. Thus, Bacchiocchi's contextual analysis is against the context. Pliny was not in the business of protecting Christians. The Christians in Bithynia were being tried not as a Jewish sect or due to associations with Judaism, but because they were perceived as suspicious in their association and activities as a *hetaeria* by the local population. Pliny, upon hearing testimony from various Christians and former Christians, concluded that Christianity was a foreign cult, a perverse superstition.[33] If they were seen as associated with Judaism, Pliny would not have been unsure of how to deal with them.[34] At least in Bithynia, the Christians had developed their own identity and were distinct from Judaism.

30. Pliny, *Letters*, 10:97.
31. Bacchiocchi, *Sabbath to Sunday*, 99.
32. Ibid., 99.
33. Wilken, *The Christians*, 22.
34. Ibid., 22.

Why the Omission?

Why was the identification of the fixed day omitted? The custom extended back prior to Pliny's account. It seems puzzling that the former Christians did not identify the day since they had nothing apparently to lose by disclosing it. The meetings had ceased after Pliny appeared as governor of Bithynia in accordance with the emperor's order and Pliny's edict. Thus, we may have a clue why the day itself was not revealed.

Given the fact that no meetings were held due to Pliny's edict, it would seem that the former believers would not hesitate to reveal the day. However, the witnesses were more concerned with revealing what went on during the meetings rather than the day itself, since the real issue was about the *activities* taking place during the assemblies. Thus, it may have been glossed over as a trivial, unimportant matter as compared to the character and events taking place at the meetings. Also, the witnesses would not wish to implicate themselves by portraying the assemblies in an otherwise innocent way. The fault or error as recorded later is rather trivial and innocent compared to the charges that were perhaps raised against them. Therefore, it is conceivable that the identification of the day itself was not seen as important by both Pliny and the former Christians because the primary focus was upon the activities taking place on the fixed day.

Was it Sunday?

Despite this probability, can identification of the day be made? It is impossible to "unambiguously" state which day is referred to.[35] However, speculation as to which day it was *not* can be arrived at with more certainty. Was it Sabbath or Sunday, or was it neither? Various reasons have been given as to why it is unlikely that the "fixed day" was Easter or the Sabbath. If it was not either, was it Sunday? It cannot be ruled out that perhaps it was the first day of the week. Whether it was weekly or bi-weekly no one can tell.

35. Bauckham, "Lord's Day," 250, fn 79.

APPENDIX 1

Even the former believers did not tell which day it was. It was concluded earlier that this may be due to the primary importance given to the activities occurring on that day. Pliny did not seem to be occupied with finding out which day it was. Pliny may not have known because the former Christians did not tell him. Bacchiocchi seems too concerned with giving Pliny's rationale for not revealing that it was Sabbath on one hand, or the reasons why he would reveal the "fixed day" as Sunday. Both are based on the supposition that Pliny knew which day it was, which cannot be certain.

Following are reasons why the "fixed day" may be referring to the first day of the week. A clue is found in the time of day in which they met. They first met "before daylight" while it was still dark. This is significant in itself. Perhaps they met before dawn to conceal their location, but this seems inconsistent when one considers that they met later on that day to "take food." Meeting at dawn is reminiscent of Christ's resurrection "at dawn on the first day of the week" (Matthew 28:1). Justin Martyr's description of a Christian worship service in Rome carries striking similarities to the one given in Pliny's letter.[36] Both contain references to observing what God's Word teaches (Pliny—"bind themselves by oath"; Justin—"exhorts to the imitation of these good things"); both mention giving to others in the group (Pliny—"not to deny a deposit"; Justin—"give what each thinks fit . . . and deposited"); each partakes in a meal, perhaps both Eucharistic (Pliny—"reassemble later to take food"; Justin—"distribution of [Eucharist meal])".

Though there is not a complete parallel between the two accounts of the worship services, the brevity of Pliny's letter does not allow for detail. Whereas Justin's letter was a believer's account, Pliny's letter was recollection by an unbeliever ignorant of Christian custom and certainly not concerned with detailing the worship routine of a group determined to be a "superstition." Furthermore, to presuppose complete uniformity in early Christian worship practices is certainly to err. There were "practical considerations, including circumstances of persecution" which "helped

---

36. Justin Martyr, *First Apology*, 67 (*The Ante-Nicene Fathers* 1:186).

to determine the times of worship."³⁷ This was certainly the case with the Christians in Bithynia.

The Christian's willingness to abandon this custom in conformity to Pliny's edict stemmed from fear and obedience. Fear of punishment was probably one factor which influenced them to obey Pliny's directive. However, apostolic instruction for submitting to the governing authorities more likely directed their conformity. As recipients of Peter's first letter, they believed they should "Submit for the Lord's sake to every authority instituted among men: whether to a king, as the supreme authority, or to governors, who are sent by him to punish those who do wrong and to commend those who do right" (1 Peter 2:13–14). Therefore, if they were observing the first day of the week it was certainly not in the vein of Sabbath observance.

Pliny's letter to Trajan cannot be used as firm proof of first day observance,³⁸ yet seems to indicate a reasonable possibility that the "fixed day" may have been the first day. Therefore, early post-apostolic practice in Bithynia may indicate first day gathering. Pliny's letter weighs in as "evidence that Christians in [Pliny's] time did worship on Sunday."³⁹ Furthermore, the evidence seems to strongly indicate the "fixed day" does not refer to the Sabbath. If it was not the Sabbath, only one other primary alternative remains: the first day of the week observed as a Christian day of worship, yet not as a rest day.⁴⁰

---

37. Bauckham, "Lord's Day," 239; van Beeck, "Worship of Christians," 125.
38. Bauckham, "Lord's Day," 250, fn 79.
39. Ibid., 250, fn 79.
40. There is general recognition that Sunday was not originally observed as a Sabbath or rest day. The letter of Pliny may be taken as evidence for this position, though no explicit statement is made in the letter that Christians worked during the "fixed day." However, there is strong implication this was probably the case. "Our study of the origins of the Lord's Day has given no hint of properly sabbatical associations; for the earliest Christians it was not a substitute for the Sabbath nor a day of rest nor related in any way to the fourth commandment" (Bauckham, "Lord's Day," 240).

APPENDIX 2

A RESPONSE TO RANKO STEFANOVIC'S "'THE LORD'S DAY' OF REVELATION 1:10 IN THE CURRENT DEBATE" *ANDREWS UNIVERSITY SEMINARY STUDIES* 49.2 (2011) 261–284.

THE enigmatic phrase "The Lord's Day" of Revelation 1:10 continues to challenge scholars of the book of Revelation and investigators of the origin of the Lord's Day. The fact that the phrase appears nowhere else in the canon of the New Testament presents the greatest challenge to interpreting the reference of the passage. Dr. Ranko Stefanovic has offered an update on the discussion of this passage in his 2011 article, "'The Lord's Day' of Revelation 1:10 in the Current Debate," which assesses scholarly investigations of the passage over the past fifty years and provides his own interpretation of the phrase in Revelation 1:10. Dr. Stefanovic has provided a valuable resource to researchers by updating the status of the current debate on Revelation 1:10 and incorporating the relevant interpretations of "The Lord's Day" into one resource. For that service all should be grateful.

The purpose of this study is to assess Dr. Stefanovic's interpretation of "The Lord's Day" in Revelation 1:10 and his final conclusions.

The Difficulties

Dr. Stefanovic identifies some difficulties involved in interpreting "The Lord's Day" in Revelation 1:10.[1]

1. "The exact phrase in Greek occurs nowhere else in the NT, LXX, or in early Christian writings (coinciding with the time of the writing of Revelation)... [and] Christian sources contemporaneous with Revelation are not particularly helpful."
2. "There is no occurrence of the adjective (*kuriakos*)in the LXX."
3. "The context does not give any indication, or even a hint, regarding which day of the week the text is referring to."

Analysis of Difficulties

The absence of *kyriake hemera* elsewhere in the New Testament may create a difficulty for interpreting the phrase, but its uniqueness may indicate a possible solution. This is bolstered by the lack of a corollary usage and reference in the Septuagint. In other words, the absence of any prior usage of the phrase in both the Septuagint and New Testament indicates the reference is to something new and without historical precedent. The sole usage of *kyriake hemera* in Revelation 1:10 indicate a new reference to a particular day. Further support for this is provided by the phrase for "the day of the Lord" in the Septuagint, *h᾽ hēmera tou kuriou*. Those who support the reference in Revelation 1:10 as another or variant way of saying "the day of the Lord" face the difficulty of explaining why John would use a different formulation from the common one used in the LXX. As pointed out by Bauckham,

"In this case, the term is not simply interchangeable with (*h᾽ hēmera tou kuriou*), since by long established usage the latter referred to the eschatological Day of the Lord. Thus if early Christians wished to call the first day of the week after their (*kyrios*), they could not use the term (*h᾽ hēmera tou kuriou*) without ambiguity

---

1. Stefanovic, "Current Debate," 261.

APPENDIX 2

and confusion."[2] Beale adds, "However, *kuriakos* is never used of the 'Day of the Lord' in the LXX, NT, or early fathers. This is not a fatal objection, but it puts the burden of proof on those arguing for the 'Day of the Lord' view."[3] Finally, Rordorf makes the point, "Despite the similarity of the designations *kuriakē hēmera* and *hˋ hēmera tou kuriou*, however, their difference is in this instance more important than their similarity."[4] Also, if the two phrases are to be identified, "why did not Revelation 1:10 use for the 'last day' the name customary in the Septuagint and in the New Testament, namely, the 'day of the Lord'?"[5]

Another indication of the expression's uniqueness is its association with Roman imperial matters during and prior to the time of Revelation 1:10.[6] While it was formerly believed that *kyriakē* was a term coined for Christian usage, it had a secular usage preceding Christian adoption of it for its association with Christ. "Thus it is not difficult to see how the word was adopted by early Christians to mean 'belonging to the Lord' Jesus Christ as a part of a resistance against emperor worship."[7] Importantly, *kyriakē* being a term "not in common secular usage except with reference to the emperor" (Bauckham 222), would seem to indicate that a narrow imperial secular usage rolled over to a distinctly Christian term associated with the Lordship of Jesus Christ and connected to a particular day (*kuriakē hēmera*). In other words, *kuriakē hēmera* became a technical term for a particular day rather than another way of referring to an already existing usage (such as "the day of the Lord").[8]

---

2. Bauckham, "Lord's Day," 225.
3. Beale, *Revelation*, 203.
4. Rordorf, *Sunday*, 208.
5. Ibid., 208; cf. Aune, *Revelation*, 1:84; Mounce, *Revelation*, 56, fn. 10.
6. Bauckham, "Lord's Day," 222; Aune, *Revelation*, 1:83.
7. Stefanovic, "Current Debate," 262.
8. Osborne, *Revelation*, 84; Mounce, *Revelation*, 55.

Literal or Figurative

Stefanovic argues that a figurative meaning of "the Lord's Day" as the eschatological Day of the Lord should not be dismissed easily. He points out the following contextual considerations. (1) "The text does not state that John was on Patmos on the Lord's Day when he received the vision, but rather that *while* he was on Patmos he came to be *in the Spirit on the Lord's Day*."[9] (2) "With regard to the usage of the expression *en pneumati*, John is consistent throughout the book; the other three subsequent occurrences of *in the Spirit* (4:2; 17:3; 21:10) refer to a symbolic rather than a literal time/place."[10] (3) Therefore, "If, in Rev 1:10, a specific, literal time is intended, it would be inconsistent with the rest of the book" (278).

Finally, (4) "The major flaw in the eschatological-day-of-the-Lord argument is that John does not use the common OT phrases ('day of the Lord') . . . in 1:10, but rather ('the Lord's Day')."[11] Evidence used to question this assertion is: (a) "One might argue that John could have taken the familiar OT terms and rephrased them."[12] (b) Citing Richard Bauckham's study of the language used relative to *kuriakos*, it is argued that "This suggests that John's use of the adjective *kyriakē* ('the *Lord's Day*'), rather than the noun *kurios* in the genitive case ('the day *of the Lord*'), does not make a substantive change in meaning."[13] (c) "The basic difference between the two phrases in both cases is simply a matter of emphasis. When the emphasis is placed on the word 'Lord,' then the noun in the genitive case (*kurios*) is used; however, when the emphasis is placed on the word 'day,' then the adjective (*kyriakē*) with a qualifying noun is used."[14] (d) The conclusion is that John possibly used "the Lord's Day" instead of "the day of the Lord" to emphasize to

9. Stefanovic, "Current Debate," 277.
10. Ibid.
11. Ibid., 278.
12. Ibid.
13. Ibid.
14. Ibid., 278-79.

the reader "that he was transported in vision into the context of the *parousia* and the events leading toward it."[15] (e) Therefore, it is argued that it is "plausible that, in Rev 1:10, the phrase (*kyriakē hemēra*) is used as one of several designations for the day of the *parousia*."[16]

Assessment of Arguments

I will now respond to each of these points in turn.

1. "The text does not state that John was on Patmos on the Lord's Day when he received the vision, but rather that *while* he was on Patmos he came to be *in the Spirit on the Lord's Day*."[17]

   Revelation 1:10 literally reads "I was in the Spirit on the Lord's Day." The time of being in Spirit for John was on the Lord's Day, not that he saw the time (the Lord's Day) while in Spirit. The text clearly puts the time of the vision as separate from the vision itself. The text states the day of the vision, not a vision of the day. The in the spirit experience occurred on the Lord's Day, not that the Lord's Day was the spiritual experience. If the "Lord's Day" reference is symbolic, then why did John not say "While in Spirit I saw the Lord's Day" or "I was in Spirit *at* the Lord's Day." It is suggested that the attention of the expression "I was in the Spirit on the Lord's Day" is focused on "I was in the Spirit" and not upon "on the Lord's Day." Attention is drawn to the state of being in the Spirit, while the reference to the Lord's Day is declarative of the time of the vision, not the content of the vision. The content of the vision actually begins in v. 12, "And when I turned I saw . . . " Prior to this, John had entered the state of being "in the Spirit" (v. 10), but the content of the experience (vision) began in v. 12. In vs. 10–11, John received instructions of what he was to do with the contents of his vision (write down and send to the seven churches).

---

15. Ibid., 279.
16. Ibid.
17. Ibid., 277.

"We find John first recording in vision Christ's message of blessing and reproof to the seven churches of Asia Minor."[18]

The location of the vision (Patmos) has nothing to do with the vision itself. It merely sets the stage of where the vision occurred. To state "but rather that *while* he was on Patmos he came to be *in the Spirit on the Lord's Day*" does not make the "Lord's Day" expression symbolic. The context surrounding Revelation 1:10 sets the stage *where* the vision occurred (i.e., Patmos, v. 9), *why* John was there (the "word of God and the testimony of Jesus", v. 9), *who* was on Patmos (John, v. 9), *when* he received the vision (the Lord's Day, v. 10), the *instructions* prior to the vision (to write down what he saw, v. 11), the *recipients* of the scroll (the seven churches, v. 11), and *what* John saw (vs. 12–18). John prefaced the vision with literal details staging the vision itself, though the vision was symbolic. The vision began in v. 12 when John turned around to "see the voice that was speaking" and he "saw seven golden lamp-stands" and "someone 'like a son of man'" (v. 13a).

The vision John had should help to identify and confirm whether the "Lord's Day" in v. 10 refers to the "day of the Lord." It is very clear that John did not see the "Lord's Day" or the events occurring on the "Lord's Day," but *heard* a voice instructing him to write down what he was to see in the vision (vs. 10b–11). "The voice like a trumpet instructs John to commit to writing what he is about to see."[19] The vision that begins in v. 12 actually does not end until the end of chapter 3 of Revelation.[20] "It is only with the 'after these things' of 4:1 that this inaugural vision is ended. This brings a strong literary unity to 1:12—3:22 and highlights the extent to which the Christological vision of 1:12–20 prepares for the letters themselves."[21]

What did John see? He saw the resurrected and glorified Christ (vs. 12–18) instructing John to "Write, therefore, what you have seen, what is now and what will take place later" (v. 19).

18. Ringer, "Saturday or Sunday?" 4.
19. Mounce, *Revelation*, 56; cf. Beale, *Revelation*, 203.
20. Osborne, *Revelation*, 85.
21. Ibid.

The vision in vs. 12–18 pictures Christ as judge and the one who holds the "keys of death and Hades." However, the picture is of Christ as judge, not of Christ exercising judgment as on the "day of the Lord." The thrust of 1:12–19 is to declare the deity of Christ ("Therefore, a major purpose is to establish the deity of Christ."[22]). The confirmation of Christ's deity is his bodily resurrection (vs. 17–18). God's sovereignty is "extended to Christ" and emphasized His eternality (Osborne 95). "What was said of God in Isaiah and Rev 1:8 is now applied to Christ because of his death and resurrection, which has placed him in his exalted office. He possesses the same transcendent attribute as God."[23]

There is a connection between when John saw the vision and the contents of the vision. The content of the vision after 1:10 closes with the resurrected Christ (1:18). The connection is the resurrection of Christ as testimony and verification of His supremacy and eternality as judge, priest, and God, and the time John saw the vision—the Lord's Day. John did not see the day of the resurrection in 1:10, but on that day saw a vision of the resurrected Lord of all creation who is God and which the day of the resurrection confirmed—the Lord's Day. Is it not interesting that John saw the resurrected Christ in a vision on the Lord's Day?

Another contextual consideration supporting the "Lord's Day" reference being not descriptive of the "day of the Lord" is 1:18. The context of the entire vision of Revelation 1:11–18 is to establish the deity of Christ in several manifestations. Furthermore, as God, Christ has complete supremacy and victory over death and evil. "Mainly, Christ through his death and resurrection has defeated the powers of evil (the twin forces of 'Death and Hades') and gained control over them... In the NT, 'key' in an eschatological text always has the idea of power or authority over a thing... Thus here he has overcome and gained mastery over the cosmic forces."[24] The focus of John is to establish the "credentials" of Christ as God, not describe the work of Christ at the "day of the Lord."

22. Ibid., 94.
23. Beale, *Revelation*, 213.
24. Osborne 96; cf. Beale 214–215.

John's vision is to demonstrate who Jesus is, not what he does on a particular day. The importance of the Lord's Day reference in 1:10 is the day of the resurrection is truly the *Lord's Day* because on that day Christ defeated death and sin which is described in the vision received on that day. "There is nothing in the context of Revelation 1:10–11 to suggest that John first saw the final Day of Judgment."[25]

2. "With regard to the usage of the expression (*en pneumati*), John is consistent throughout the book; the other three subsequent occurrences of *in the Spirit* (4:2; 17:3; 21:10) refer to a symbolic rather than a literal time/place."[26]

The point with regard to usage of the expression "in the Spirit" in other passages of Revelation as indicating "a symbolic rather than a literal time/place" is overstated and off course. What is consistent with John's usage is that the expression "in the Spirit" describes the condition he enters that enables him to see the vision. What he sees is symbolic, yet the "in the Spirit" experience is literal. The other expressions have nothing to do with the timing of the vision or the literal time or place of the vision. All this is to say the experience of being "in the Spirit" may or may not be connected to the time they occurred. In the case of 1:10, a time is given—"on the Lord's Day"—yet the visions are not of the day itself. Beale states with respect to 4:2 that being ushered into the spiritual, timeless dimension of God's heavenly council means that the time of the events that John sees in vision may be difficult to determine precisely. Some of the symbols may be descriptive symbolism in that they portray what has taken place up to the present. Or they may contain determinative symbolism predicting what will come to pass. We have observed how all the visions from 6:1 to 22:5 flow out of the vision in chs. 4–5. Therefore, they all probably have a mixture of past, present, and future elements.[27]

There is no indication from the other passages where "in the Spirit" appears that they occurred at another time than the first

---

25. Ringer, "Saturday or Sunday?" 4.
26. Stefanovic, "Current Debate," 277.
27. Beale, *Revelation*, 319.

APPENDIX 2

vision John received starting in 1:10. It is possible, but not determinative, to think the "in the Spirit" experiences in Revelation 1:10, 4:2, 17:3, and 21:10, all occurred on the Lord's Day, because the contents of all the visions was not about the "day of the Lord." "There is no indication of time, and it is impossible to know if there was a period between the visions."[28] The expression "in the Spirit" "points to a Holy Spirit-sent visionary experience in which God reveals his mysteries."[29] The visions were literal experiences occurring at a literal place, yet were symbolic in content. To use the symbolic nature of the visions to make the time of the vision symbolic is an assumption and overstated. Therefore, to state that "If, in Rev 1:10, a specific, literal time is intended, it would be inconsistent with the rest of the book" is off course. There is no inconsistency in reading "the Lord's Day" of 1:10 as referring to a literal day unless one assumes that because the visions are symbolic in content automatically means the time of the vision is as well. The "in the Spirit" experience is a literal experience and the visions are symbolic. Likewise, the day(s) the visions were received is literal as well.

3. Therefore, "If, in Rev 1:10, a specific, literal time is intended, it would be inconsistent with the rest of the book."[30]

The visions were literal experiences occurring at a literal place yet were symbolic in content. To use the symbolic nature of the visions to make the time of the vision symbolic is an assumption and overstated. There is no inconsistency in reading "the Lord's Day" of 1:10 as referring to a literal day unless one assumes that because the visions are symbolic in content automatically means the time of the vision is as well. The "in the Spirit" experience is a literal experience and the vision's content is symbolic. Likewise, the day the visions were received is literal as well. The "Lord's Day" in 1:10 is the only reference to the historical time the visions occurred. This

---

28. Osborne, *Revelation*, 223.
29. Ibid., 225.
30. Stefanovic, "Current Debate," 278.

adds weight to the argument that the visions were not about a day (Day of the Lord) but referred to the day the visions were received. Stefanovic ignores the fact the Revelation is not only a series of visions with figurative and symbolic significance, but these visions are set in a narrative that sets the stage for the visions. Therefore, there is no inconsistency in the relationship between the literal setting and narrative of the visions.

4. "The major flaw in the eschatological-day-of-the-Lord argument is that John does not use the common OT phrases ("the day of the Lord") . . . in 1:10, but rather ("the Lord's Day")" (278). Also, "John could have taken the familiar OT terms and rephrased them."[31]

This seems unlikely as Revelation would be the only place that John uses *kuriakē hēmera* as the "day of the Lord." Why would John use a new phrase to describe the Parousia rather than the standard phrase common in the LXX? The burden of proof lies with those seeking to explain this unique phraseology as applying to the Parousia. The position that the language similar to *kuriakos* "suggests that John's use of the adjective *kyriakē* ('the Lord's Day'), rather than the noun *kurios* in genitive case ('the day *of the Lord*'), does not make a substantive change in meaning."[32] Citation of Richard Bauckham is used to make this case. However, Bauckham asserts "we have no evidence of the adjective *kuriake* used of the eschatological day, whereas it is regularly used for the day of the week."[33] The difference between the two expressions is more marked than the similarity. The suggestion that there is not a substantive difference between the two expressions is not an indisputable fact. The question persists, why did John not use the standard phrase for the "day of the Lord" when the expression was known from prior usage throughout biblical history? Why would John use another expression for a day most clearly understood by "the day of the Lord"? The impression one gets by the argumentation

31. Ibid.
32. Ibid.
33. Richard Bauckham, personal email correspondence with author.

that attempts to make the two phrases say the same thing is there is "special pleading" occurring to make it so. A rule of thumb is simply the more argumentation needed to make two different expressions the same meaning testifies to the difference.

Stefanovic concludes that John possibly changed the expressions because he wanted "to inform the reader that he was transported in vision into the context of the *parousia* and the events leading toward it."[34] However, as Bauckham points out, it makes no sense "of John's visions to think that he was already transported to the last day at the beginning of the narrative of the book. The initial vision of Christ and the messages to the churches in chs 1–3 is not set in the future, but in the present. His later references to 'the great day of God' (16:14) show that he thought of this day as coming at the end of the eschatological events that he foresees in chs 5–19." In addition, S.R. Llewelyn states that the verb *'was'* (*egenomēn*) used in Revelation 1:10 is also used in Revelation 4:2, 8:1, and 11:13; in each of these cases he notes "The time reference is to when the event occurred. By analogy, the reference in Revelation 1:10 must be to the time when the seer had his spiritual experience. Second, if the writer wished to indicate a future time towards which he was transferred in the vision, then one would have expected a prepositional phrase in the accusative . . . rather than one in the dative."[35]

Conclusions

Dr. Stefanovic has concluded that Revelation 1:10 carries a dual reference that uses the "Lord's Day" as referring to both the seventh day Sabbath and the eschatological day of the Lord.[36] However, it is believed enough evidence has been presented to dispute the equating of "the Lord's Day" with "the day of the Lord." The fact John did not use the "day of the Lord" language, but rather "the Lord's Day,"

---

34. Stefanovic, "Current Debate," 279.
35. Llewelyn, "Use of Sunday," 222.
36. Stefanovic, "Current Debate," 284.

testifies to an important distinction between the two expressions referring to separate times. Consider the following argument,

> It is certainly understandable why Christians who gathered on the first day of the week to worship would need to choose a name for that day that indicated that it was given over to remembrance of Christ's resurrection until he returned. They could not use the 'Day of the Lord' lest it be confused with the final Day of Judgment. This could account for their distinctive use of (the Lord's Day) to refer to the day of Christ's resurrection. *Kyriakē* was already in use in the first century to refer to the Imperial authority, administration, and the treasury of Caesar. In addition, Caesar was worshipped by the Romans as a god. *Kyriakē* would seem to be an ideal word with which to ascribe true Lordship to Jesus Christ who not only created all things but who also rose from the dead on the first day of the week.[37]

The context of Revelation's setting is vital on this point. By 90 C.E., Christians could choose an expression for the day of Christ's resurrection that would express it in a unique manner not previously done. It was clearly understood in the province of Asia and the seven churches addressed in Revelation 1–3. Of major importance is the fact that the expression "the Lord's Day" would become the prominent expression to the day of Christ's resurrection certainly in the later second century and perhaps earlier.

The fact *kyriakē hemēra* ("the Lord's Day) is not used prior to Revelation 1:10 points to it as a new expression for the church to refer to a specific day of the week. This is probably connected to the immediate context of the book of Revelation itself.

---

37. Ringer, "Saturday or Sunday?" 12.

BIBLIOGRAPHY

The Ante-Nicene Fathers: Translations of the Writings of the Fathers Down to A.D. 325. 10 vols. Edited by Alexander Roberts and James Donaldson. 1885–1887. Repr., Grand Rapids: Eerdmans, 1987.
Archer, Gleason L. *Encyclopedia of Bible Difficulties.* Grand Rapids: Zondervan, 1982.
Aune, David. *Revelation.* Dallas: Word, 1997.
Bacchiocchi, Samuele. *From Sabbath to Sunday.* Rome: Gregorian University Press, 1977.
———. "The Rise of Sunday Observance in Early Christianity." In *The Sabbath in Scripture and History.* Washington, D.C.: Review and Herald, 1982.
———. *The Time of the Crucifixion and Resurrection.* Berrien Springs: Biblical Perspectives, 1985.
Bauckham, Richard. "The Lord's Day." In *From Sabbath to Lord's Day*, edited by D. A. Carson, 221–50. Grand Rapids: Zondervan, 1982.
———. "Sabbath and Sunday in the Post-Apostolic Church." In *From Sabbath to Lord's Day*, edited by D. A. Carson, 251–98. Grand Rapids: Zondervan, 1982.
Beale, G. K. *The Book of Revelation.* Grand Rapids: Eerdmans, 1999.
Beasley-Murray, George R. *Jesus and the Kingdom of God.* Grand Rapids: Eerdmans, 1986.
Bratcher, Robert G. and Howard A. Hatton. *A Handbook on the Revelation to John.* New York: United Bible Societies, 1993.
Brown, Raymond E. *The Gospel According to John XIII–XXI.* Garden City: Doubleday, 1970.
Bullinger, E. W. *The Lord's Day.* Brookfield, WI: Bible Search Publications, N.D.
Carson, D.A. *The Gospel According to John.* Grand Rapids: Eerdmans, 1991.
———. "Introduction." In *From Sabbath to Lord's Day*, edited by D. A. Carson, 13–19. Grand Rapids: Zondervan, 1982.
Conzelmann, Hans. *The Acts of the Apostles.* Philadelphia: Fortress, 1987.
De Vries, S. J. "Day." In *The Interpreter's Dictionary of the Bible* 1, edited by George Arthur Buttrick. Nashville: Abingdon, 1962.
Delling, Gerhard. "Day." In *Theological Dictionary of the New Testament* 2, edited by Gerhard Kittel. Grand Rapids: Eerdmans, 1964.
Dods, Marcus. *The Expositor's Bible: The First Epistle to the Corinthians.* Hartford: S. S. Scranton, 1889.

Dugmore, C. W. "Lord's Day and Easter." In *Neotestamentica et Patristica. Supplement to Novum Testamentum* 6:272–81. Leiden: Brill, 1962.

Dunn, James D. G. *Jesus, Paul and the Law*. Louisville: Westminster, 1988.

Ellison, H. L. "Sunday." In *The New International Dictionary of the Christian Church*, edited by J. D. Douglas. Grand Rapids: Zondervan, 1978.

Feneberg, W. "Third." In *Exegetical Dictionary of the New Testament* 3, edited by Horst Balz and Gerhard Schneider. Grand Rapids: Eerdmans, 1982.

Geraty, Lawrence T. "The Pascha and the Origin of Sunday Observance," Andrews University Seminary Studies 3 (1965) 87–90.

Goppelt, Leonhard, *A Commentary on I Peter*. Grand Rapids: Eerdmans, 1993.

Guelich, Robert A. *Mark 1–8:26*. Dallas: Word, 1989.

Habermas, Gary R. *The Verdict of History*. Nashville: Thomas Nelson, 1988.

Harris, Murray J. *Raised Immortal*. Grand Rapids: Eerdmans, 1983.

Harris, Ralph W., Ed. *The Complete Biblical Library* 12. Springfield, MO: World Library P, 1986.

———., Ed. *The Complete Biblical Library* 14. Springfield, MO: World Library P, 1986.

Hemer, C. J. "τρεις." In *The New International Dictionary of New Testament Theology* 2:686–87, edited by Colin Brown. Grand Rapids: Zondervan, 1976.

Hendriksen, William. "The Gospel of Mark." In *New Testament Commentary*. Grand Rapids: Baker, 1975.

Hoehner, Harold W. *Chronological Aspects of the Life of Christ*. Grand Rapids: Zondervan, 1977.

Horton, Stanley M. *The New Testament Study Bible: Matthew*. In The Complete Biblical Library 2, edited by. Ralph W. Harris. Springfield: World Library Press, 1986.

Jewett, Paul K. *The Lord's Day*. Grand Rapids: Eerdmans, 1971.

Justin Martyr. "The First Apology of Justin." In *The Ante-Nicene Fathers* 1, edited by Alexander Roberts and James Donaldson. Grand Rapids: Eerdmans, 1987.

Kerr, Hugh T., ed. *Readings in Christian Thought*. Nashville: Abingdon, 1966.

Knox, John. "Pliny and 1 Peter: A Note on 1 Peter 4:14–16 and 3:15." *Journal of Biblical Literature* 72 (1953) 187–89.

Kurtright, Steve. "The Technical Use of the Word 'Preparation' in the Gospels." In *Ministerial Forum* (Winter 1991) 32–33.

Lamsa, George M. *New Testament Light*. San Francisco: Harper and Row, 1960.

Lenski, R. C. H. *The Interpretation of the Acts of the Apostles*. Minneapolis: Augsburg, 1934.

Lincoln, A. T. "From Sabbath to Lord's Day: A Biblical and Theological Perspective." In *From Sabbath to Lord's Day*, edited by D. A. Carson, 343–412. Grand Rapids: Zondervan, 1982.

Lindsell, Harold. "After Three Days and Three Nights." *Christianity Today* (April 1977) 14–16.

Llewelyn, S. R. "The Use of Sunday for Meetings of Believers in the New Testament." *Novum Testamentum* 43.3 (2001) 205–23.
Lohse, Eduard. "Pentecost." In *Theological Dictionary of the New Testament* 6, edited by Gerhard Friedrich. Grand Rapids: Eerdmans, 1968.
Longenecker, Richard N. "Acts." In *The Expositor's Bible Commentary* 9. Grand Rapids: Zondervan, 1981.
Marshall, I. Howard. *Acts*. Grand Rapids: Eerdmans, 1980.
McArthur, A. A. *The Evolution of the Christian Year*. London: SCM Press, 1953.
McArthur, H. K. "On the Third Day." *New Testament Studies* 18 (1971) 81–86.
McDowell, Josh. *The Resurrection Factor*. San Bernardino: Here's Life, 1981.
Morris, Leon. *The Gospel According to Matthew*. Grand Rapids: Eerdmans, 1992.
Mounce, Robert H. *The Book of Revelation*, rev ed. Grand Rapids: Eerdmans, 1998.
Nolland, John. *Luke 18:35—24:53*. Dallas: Word, 1993.
Odom, Robert L. "Sabbath and Sunday in Early Christianity." In *The Sabbath in Scripture and History*, edited by Kenneth A. Strand. Washington, D.C.: Review and Herald, 1977, 73.
Osborne, Grant R. *Revelation*. Grand Rapids: Baker, 2002.
Phillips, John. *Exploring Acts: An Expository Commentary*. Grand Rapids: Kregel, 1986.
Pliny, *Letters and Panegyricus* II, Books VIII–X. Translated by Betty Radice. Cambridge: Harvard University Press, 1969.
Polhill, John B. *Acts*. Nashville: Broadman, 1992.
Pope, M. H. "Number." In *The Interpreter's Dictionary of the Bible* 3, edited by George Arthur Buttrick. Nashville: Abingdon, 1962.
Riesenfeld, Harald. *The Gospel Tradition*. Philadelphia: Fortress, 1970.
Ringer, Wes. "Should Christians Worship on Saturday or Sunday? 'The Lord's Day': An Analysis of the Meaning of the Phrase in Revelation 1:10." www.godandscience.org/doctrine/lords_day.pdf.
Robinson, John A. T. "Resurrection." In *The Interpreter's Dictionary of the Bible* 5, edited by George Arthur Buttrick. Nashville: Abingdon, 1962.
Rordorf, Willy. *Sunday*. Philadelphia: Westminster, 1968.
Specht, Walter F. "Sunday in the New Testament." In *The Sabbath in Scripture and History*, edited by Kenneth A. Strand. Washington, D.C.: Review and Herald, 1982.
Stefanovic, Ranko. "'The Lord's Day' of Revelation 1:10 in the Current Debate." *Andrews University Seminary Studies* 49.2 (2011) 261–84.
Stott, John R. W. *The Spirit, the Church, and the World*. Downers Grove: InterVarsity, 1990.
Stott, Wilfrid. "A Note on the Word Κυριακή in Rev. i. 10." *New Testament Studies* 12 (1965) 70–75.
———. "σάββατον." In *The New International Dictionary of New Testament Theology* 3:405–11, edited by Colin Brown. Grand Rapids: Zondervan, 1978.

———. "κυριακή." In *The New International Dictionary of New Testament Theology* 3:411–12, edited by Colin Brown, Editor. Grand Rapids: Zondervan, 1978.

Strand, Kenneth A. "Another Look at 'Lord's Day' in the Early Church and in Rev. 1:10." *New Testament Studies* 13 (1967) 174–81.

———. "From Sabbath to Sunday in the Early Christian Church: A Review of Some Recent Literature." *Andrews University Seminary Studies* 17.1 (Spring 1979) 85–104.

———. "The 'Lord's Day' in the Second Century." In *The Sabbath in Scripture and History*, edited by Kenneth A. Strand. Washington, DC: Review and Herald, 1982.

The Duration of Jesus' Entombment. Denver: Bible Advocate, n.d.

The Time Element in the Crucifixion and Resurrection of Christ. Denver: Bible Advocate, n.d.

Thiele, F. "κατασκευάζω." In *The New International Dictionary of New Testament Theology* 3:118–20, edited by Colin Brown. Grand Rapids: Zondervan, 1978.

Throckmorton, B. H. "Third Day." In *The Interpreter's Dictionary of the Bible* 4, edited by George Arthur Buttrick. Nashville: Abingdon, 1962.

Turner, Max M. B. "The Sabbath, Sunday, and the Law in Luke/Acts." In *From Sabbath to Lord's Day*, edited by D. A. Carson, 99–157. Grand Rapids: Zondervan, 1982.

van Beeck, Franz Jozef. "The Worship of Christians in Pliny's Letter." *Studia Liturgica* 18 (1988) 12131.

Watt, R. J. G. "On the Third Day." *The Expository Times* 88:1 (1977) 276.

Wilken, Robert L. *The Christians as the Romans Saw Them.* New Haven: Yale University Press, 1984.

www.ingramcontent.com/pod-product-compliance
Lightning Source LLC
Chambersburg PA
CBHW070918160426
43193CB00011B/1505